PRO
HOCKEY HEROES
OF TODAY

Exciting profiles of 24 top hockey stars: scoring leaders
Phil Esposito and Bobby Hull, defensemen Bobby Orr
and Brad Park, goalies Tony Esposito and Bernie Parent,
and many others. More than 100 action photographs
depict the speed, the grace and the toughness of the men
who help make hockey the fastest and fastest-growing
sport in North America.

illustrated with photographs

PRO
HOCKEY
HEROES
OF TODAY

BY BILL LIBBY

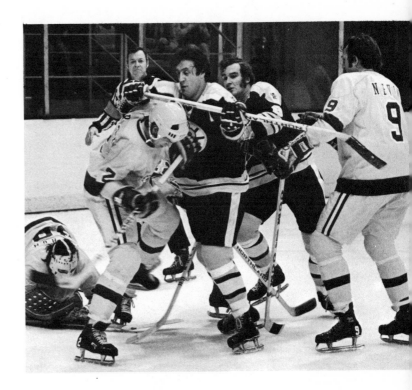

Random House / New York

Acknowledgments

The author wishes to thank Jack Kent Cooke, Larry Regan, Jake Milford, Dick White and Mike Hope of the Los Angeles Kings and the owners, managers, coaches and publicists of all the clubs in hockey who have helped this writer pursue his passion for this sport.

He wishes also to thank Ken McKenzie and Charlie Halpin of *The Hockey News*, in whose pages the seeds of many of these stories sprouted, as well as all of the writers whose work has contributed to his knowledge of the game and its players.

Finally, and most importantly, he wishes to thank all of the players who have taken the trouble to give the author interviews and information in both the best and worst of times and without whom we have nothing.

Copyright © 1974 by Random House, Inc.
All rights reserved under International and Pan-American Copyright Conventions.
Published in the United States by Random House, Inc., New York,
and simultaneously in Canada by Random House of Canada Limited, Toronto.

Text design: Harriett Banner
Jacket design: Murray M. Herman

Library of Congress Cataloging in Publication Data
Libby, Bill.   Pro hockey heroes of today.   (Landmark giant #25)
SUMMARY: Profiles of twenty-four hockey stars including goalies,
scoring leaders, and defensemen.   1. Hockey—Biography—Juvenile literature.
[1. Hockey—Biography] I. Title. GV848.5.A1L52 1974   796.9′62′0922 [B]   [920]
ISBN 0-394-82761-9   74-4929   ISBN 0-394-92761-3 (lib. bdg.)

Manufactured in the United States of America   1 2 3 4 5 6 7 8 9 0

For Sharon, my wife, who brought
me all the good things in life.

Contents

Introduction

The 24 hockey players chosen for this book are not the 24 highest scorers or the 24 highest-paid or even the 24 most colorful. They have been chosen to represent a cross-section of top performers with varied skills from varied backgrounds whose accomplishments on the ice and lives off the ice are the most interesting to be found in this fascinating sport.

There are explosive scorers like Phil Esposito and Bobby Hull, revolutionary defensemen like Bobby Orr and Brad Park, traditional defensemen like Terry Harper, specialists like Dave Keon and great goaltenders like Tony Esposito and Bernie Parent. There are veterans like Hull and Frank Mahovlich and rising youngsters like Bobby Clarke and Rick Martin. Some are colorful, some conservative. But all deserve their places in this book for great performances in professional hockey's big leagues.

Canada is the cradle of hockey in North America, and all the stars in this book grew up there. Still, they come from many backgrounds. Jim Neilson is a North American Indian; Stan Mikita was born in Czechoslovakia; Yvan Cournoyer, Gil Perreault, J. C. Tremblay and others are French-Canadians. They play for 14 teams scattered all across the continent, representing both the National Hockey League and the World Hockey Association.

Many other stars might have been selected for this volume. We regret having to leave out a number of deserving performers. We can only hope that readers will find some of their favorites among the 24 who were chosen and will enjoy this portrait of a great game and its heroes.

BILL LIBBY

PRO
HOCKEY HEROES
OF TODAY

Cleveland Crusader goalie Gerry Cheevers makes a save in the 1973 WHA playoffs.

Gerry Cheevers

There are nights when the puck seems as small as a golf ball to a goaltender. Gerry Cheevers, now a top goalie for the Cleveland Crusaders in the World Hockey Association (WHA), had such a night during his rookie season in December of 1966. Playing for the Boston Bruins, then a weak team in the National Hockey League (NHL), Cheevers seemed to let every shot get by him and into the net. "I was like a duck in a shooting gallery," he recalled. He lost, 10-2.

Afterwards he was sitting in the Boston Bruins' dressing room when manager Hap Emms charged in to complain about the team's play and about Cheevers in particular. "Damn it," Emms shouted, "what happened out there?"

Cheevers looked the manager straight in the eye and said, "Roses are red, violets are blue, they got ten, we only got two."

Emms started to sputter in amazement. How does a manager handle a goalie who just gave up ten goals and then gives a wise-guy answer when asked about it? Years later, Cheevers claimed that his attitude was important to being a successful goalie.

"It's only a game," he said. "It's my job. It pays me well and I want to do well at it. But I'm not going to make myself sick over it. I do the best I can. If it's not good enough, the next time I try to do better."

Fortunately for Cheevers, there also were nights when the puck appeared to be big as a balloon. On those nights it seemed to the shooters that not even the greatest shot in hockey would get by him. His most memorable moment was the sixth game of the Stanley Cup playoff finals in April of 1972. Playing for the Bruins against the New York Rangers, Gerry faced a desperate Ranger team. They needed a victory to stay alive in the series and threw everything at the visiting Bruins. Some 17,500 fans cheered for the home side and taunted the hated visitors from Boston.

With the Bruins ahead 1-0 on a goal by Bobby Orr, Cheevers did the splits to kick out one shot to the far corner, dove to catch a shot at the other corner, raced out of the net to poke a puck off an enemy stick at one point, and then fell on a puck to protect it from the flailing sticks of the Ranger attackers.

Through all three periods, Cheevers held the powerful Rangers in check, and the Bruins triumphed, 3-0, winning the Stanley Cup for the second time in three years. It was the most satisfying shutout of his career for a professional who had taken many years to gain recognition for his talents. Afterwards in the dressing room, Cheevers looked up with a happy grin and said, "The old boy is vindicated."

After his triumph, Cheevers jumped from the Bruins to the Cleveland Crusaders of the new WHA for three times his previous salary. During the 1972-73 season, he led all netminders in the league with the lowest goals-against averages in the regular season and the post-season playoffs. He was voted to the first All-Star team. Few would have predicted ten years earlier that Cheevers, then a lightly re-garded journeyman goaltender, would ever be on top of the world, earning over $200,000 a year and setting new stand-ards in one of the sport's most demanding specialties.

"No one wants to be a goaltender," Gerry Cheevers once said with a grin. "As kids, the fattest boys, poorest skaters and worst players are stuck in the net."

Yet goaltending is a truly awesome art in the pros. Burdened by twenty pounds of protective gear, the goalie must move like a cat to stop shots that may travel 100 miles per hour. He must have intense concentration, lightning reflexes and calm nerves, refusing to shy away from bullet-like shots or the menacing skates and sticks of his attackers. Most goalies even-tually suffer from nervous exhaustion—in addition to a multitude of bruises, cuts and other physical injuries. Cheevers got the bruises and cuts, but he seemed to survive the tension of goaltending, seem-ing almost cheerful about his job.

Cheevers was born December 7, 1940, in St. Catharines, Ontario, a hotbed of hockey talent near Toronto. His father, a former hockey player and lacrosse star, managed the local ice rink and coached kids' hockey teams. Gerry recalled, "I be-came a goalie because I wasn't good enough to be anything else and because my dad, who was the coach, couldn't find anyone else to play goal for our CYO team. My first game, we lost, 17-0. I'm not kidding."

But he soon showed promise and was signed by the Toronto Maple Leafs. After the climb through amateur and minor league hockey, he first joined Toronto in 1961. But the Maple Leafs had star veter-ans in the nets, and he got to play in only two games. In the next few years he bounced back and forth from the major leagues to the minors, never seeing much playing time in Toronto. Then in 1965 he was taken by Boston in the post-season intra-team draft. Each team can protect only its most valuable players, and To-ronto chose not to protect its young jour-neyman goalie, so the Bruins, then a weak team, bought Cheevers' contract. Yet even with the Bruins, he still traveled often between the majors and the minors. "I covered more ground than a stew-ardess," he later recalled. "For a while there, I had to look down at my uniform to see what team I was playing for that night. I never knew were I was. After a while, all the towns and arenas looked the same. The human yo-yo was at home anywhere."

But the Bruins were being transformed from a last-place to a first-place team. Bobby Orr arrived in 1966, and Phil Es-posito arrived in 1967. Cheevers became a regular goalie at the right time, in the 1967-68 season. For many years, pro hockey teams had used only one regular goaltender. But by '67 the schedule had lengthened, travel had increased and times were changing. Teams began to split the goaltending between two or three regulars. Cheevers divided the work with Ed Johnston, playing from 40 to 50 games a season. Along the way, Boston let such good goalies as Bernie Parent and Doug Favell go to keep the more de-pendable Cheevers.

The Big Bad Bruins, as they became known, roughed up foes and broke scor-ing records, often making six or seven or

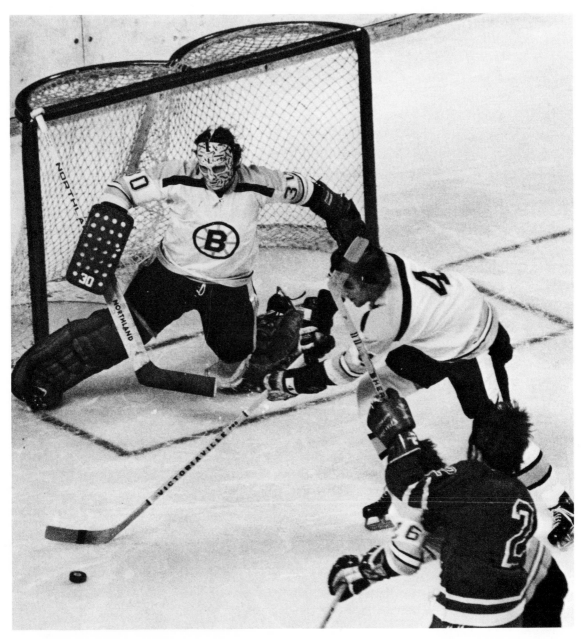

As a Bruin in 1972, Cheevers guards the net while teammate Bobby Orr (4) gets the puck.

eight goals a game. Cheevers' goals-against average was not outstanding, but with such a powerhouse offense, it didn't matter. "It's hard to take a one-sided game seriously," he shrugged. "We won, which is what mattered."

His marks were more impressive in the playoffs, where winning was less easy. Former coach Tom Johnson said, "Gerry is at his best when it counts the most. He has an unusually good disposition for a goaltender. He's a little nutty like most of them, but he doesn't throw up before games. And when the pressure builds up, he comes through in the clutch."

Like most goaltenders, Cheevers was a convenient scapegoat. When the Bruins blew big games, he was blamed. When they won them, he was overlooked. Yet in 1970, when the Bruins won their first Stanley Cup since 1939, Cheevers set a record by winning ten straight games in the playoffs. Two years later, he tended goal in a record of 32 straight games without a loss. Nevertheless, Orr, Esposito and the other Bruins got most of the attention.

At 5-foot-11 and 185 pounds, Cheevers seemed too stocky, but he was amazingly quick and agile. Some goalies had faster hands, but few could match Cheevers' skating ability. He was sometimes guilty of skating too much, straying away from his net to break up offensive plays. When he failed, he looked bad and infuriated his coaches. One coach punished him by making him play at forward. Still, his daring forays out of the net stopped many likely goals.

Cheevers could use his stick the way a jungle fighter uses a knife. He kept the path clear in front of his net by his willingness to come out and cross sticks with foes. Despite his aggressiveness, he was no fighter. "I'm the worst fighter in the world," he admitted. "There is no way I could win a fight, so I have to get my licks in before the fight starts."

Gerry started to wear a mask in 1965 after a game in which a puck hit him in the mouth and knocked out six teeth. "I put my hand to my mouth and I can still see the teeth that fell into my glove," he recalled. It took 35 stitches to close the

wound, but he went back into the game and won.

Every time a shot hit his mask, he marked the spot by sketching on stitch marks. The mask soon took on a garish monster-like appearance. "Can you imagine what my face would look like without one?" he laughs. "Those stitch marks are my medals of honor. I would be a coward without my mask now. We're at war out there and my stick and my mask are my sword and shield."

Although many goalies are quiet and withdrawn off the ice, Cheevers got a reputation as a practical joker. Once during a party at Bobby Orr's Boston restaurant, Cheevers disappeared through the revolving door into the kitchen. Moments

After tense games behind a bizarre mask . . .

. . . Gerry relaxed by training horses and playing practical jokes.

later he emerged dressed as a chef. Then he disappeared and returned as a waiter. The third time he was dressed as a waitress.

Cheevers' biggest interest outside of hockey was horse racing. He owned and raced horses and hoped to become a trainer when he retired. During the summer he spoke to banquets as a representative of a race track in Ontario.

Many hockey fans wondered why a top goalie for a championship team would jump to a new and untested league. Cheevers reminded them that professional sports are an insecure business. Even superstars can be traded, lose their edge or suffer serious injury. The Crusaders offered him a long-term contract and nearly three times the salary. In addi-

tion they lent him money to buy a house and provided a free car annually and bonuses if he and the team did well.

"It was hard to leave Boston," he said. "But there is no sentiment in sports. With Cleveland, I make a lot more money and have a lot more security. It was tough getting used to smaller crowds and less publicity, but the new league will attract attention and the crowds will grow. The new league is good for hockey. It broadens interest in the sport and opens up jobs."

The "human yo-yo" had opened up a big job for himself. With a relaxed approach and smart play and smart answers, he had become the most colorful, the most prosperous—and possibly the best—goalie in hockey.

Bobby Clarke

Sweaty and exhausted, Bobby Clarke sat in front of his locker in the lower reaches of Philadelphia's Spectrum and cried. He was a professional hockey player and tougher than most, but he was heartbroken. For the second time in three seasons his team, the Philadelphia Flyers, had lost a spot in the playoffs in the last games of the season. And this time, they had lost the critical game in the last minute. It was April of 1972, and Clarke had just completed a fine season, but that was no consolation. His team had been beaten.

"I can't believe it," he said in a soft, sorrowful voice. "It's going to be tough to live with. We'll have to bounce back from it, somehow."

Finally he straightened up, and sparks seemed to blaze from his blue eyes. "We will bounce back," he vowed.

The following season the Flyers did bounce back. Bobby Clarke had been named the youngest team captain in NHL history at 22, and he led his expansion team into second place in its division, within a few points of the long-estab-

Rough, tough competitor Bobby Clarke (16) tries to skate around Chicago's Pat Stapleton.

Two Canadiens gang up on Bobby while the Montreal goalie retrieves the puck.

lished Chicago Black Hawks. They made the playoffs with plenty to spare. Then, in the 1973-74 season, he paced Philadelphia past Chicago to the pennant with the finest record any expansion team had ever achieved.

In the fall of 1967, the National Hockey League had added six expansion teams to its six established teams, doubling in size in a single season. By 1974, six more were established. The Flyers were part of the first expansion, and like all the others, they began as a weak team, making do with declining veterans and untried young players. In the first six years after expansion, none of the new teams had come close to the Stanley Cup.

But for sparking his team near the top, Bobby Clarke was voted the Hart Trophy as the league's most valuable player. He was the first player from an expansion team honored with this most coveted of hockey awards, and the first of the new breed of young players to join the select circle of the circuit's superstars.

As he became a familiar star in the NHL, fans were shocked to learn that Clarke had diabetes, a serious sickness which can be controlled only with constant and careful care. Because of some bodily deficiency, a diabetic cannot burn the sugar he eats. If the condition is not controlled, the sugar builds up in the diabetic's blood and soon sends him into convulsions or a coma. So he must take insulin or some other drug which helps burn the sugar properly, but he must carefully balance his sugar intake and his insulin intake. He walks a tightrope—too much or too little sugar may cause loss of coordination and vision, weakness, fainting spells or even convulsions.

Bobby Clarke gave himself an injection of insulin every morning, and with the help of his wife and his doctor, he carefully controlled his diet. The team trainer gave him a Coke or several teaspoons of sugar before every game. Then the sugar he burned during games had to be replaced. Between periods he drank a half-glass of sweetened orange juice and after the final period he drank a full glass. For emergencies, the trainer carried a large supply of chocolate bars in his kit and a solution of glucose that Bobby could drink if his blood sugar reached dangerously low levels.

Another danger to the diabetic is infection. Hockey is a rough, dangerous sport. The players carry sticks and collide at great speeds. Tempers flare and fists fly. The sticks sometimes are used as weapons. The hard rubber pucks are shot at dizzying speed and sometimes strike players.

Like all hockey players, Bobby suffered his share of cuts. The tough tradition in hockey compels players to get stitched up swiftly and back into action within minutes. Clarke's cuts were carefully cleaned and dressed, but he returned to the ice as swiftly as the next player.

Bobby was embarrassed when anyone made too much of his condition. "I do everything every other player does," he said. "I play rough and expect to get roughed up in return. I want no favors. I want to be judged on my play, not on my problem. I have a problem, other players have other problems. Some have bad backs or bad knees. Some play with steel plates in their skulls. I have to do

some things to care for my problem. Other players have to do other things. Some play strapped up in braces."

Robert Earle Clarke was born August 13, 1949, in colorfully named Flin Flon, Manitoba, in sparsely populated Western Canada. Like many hockey stars, Bobby grew up where natural ice was available much of the year and the winter temperatures sank far below zero for weeks at a time.

Flin Flon is a company town of about 12,000 persons. Bobby's father and many other men in town worked for the Hudson Bay Mining and Smelting Company. For 25 years he worked as a driller 2,500 feet below ground in the copper and zinc mines. Later he became a blasting boss. It was a hard, risky profession and he preferred something else for his son.

Bobby wanted to be a hockey player almost from the time he started to skate. At the age of eight he claimed that he was nine so he could qualify for play in the pee-wee hockey program. He also played pick-up games, staying out from dawn to dusk even when it was 30 to 40 degrees below zero. "I used to tell my parents that I was going to school, but I'd go to the rink instead," he recalled with a smile. "Or I would misbehave in school and be sent home, but go to the rink instead."

Then when he was 15 he discovered he had diabetes. "I never thought of anything else but playing pro hockey. When I found out I had diabetes I wasn't frightened for my life, but for my future in hockey. I took all the tests and treatments and I was relieved when I was told I could continue to play."

In 1967-68 and '68-69 he was a sensa-

Although aggressive on the ice, Bobby seems shy and studious off the ice.

Every team passed him over in the first round. Finally in the second round Philadelphia took a chance on him. He won a position with the Flyers in his first pre-season camp and never spent a day in the minor leagues. He was brilliant from the beginning and he improved his statistics and his all-around play each of his first three seasons. In '72-73 he was most valuable player, scoring 37 goals and 67 assists for 104 points, second only to Phil Esposito, the powerful Boston Bruin veteran. And in '73-74, he came back with 35 goals and 52 assists for 87 points.

It was his all-around play that set him apart from others. The Flyers were setting all-time records for penalty minutes. That meant that the team played short-handed more than any other in the league. Bobby led one of the regular Philadelphia forward lines, but when the team was short-handed, he could show some of his special skills, "killing" the penalty with his swift-skating defense. He was especially skilled at stealing the puck while his side was short-handed and sailing in on a breakaway to score. Nothing in hockey is as demoralizing as being scored on when your team has a six-man-to-five advantage.

Clarke usually spent more than half of every 60-minute game on the ice—10 or 15 minutes more than the average forward. Although the teams played a tough schedule of 80 to 100 games including pre-season and post-season games, he seldom seemed to tire. He missed only one regular-season game his first four seasons. Once when he was suffering a weak spell, he had to be threatened with fines to keep him away from practices.

Fred Shero, the Flyer coach, said, "He

tion as an amateur with the Flin Flon Bombers in the Western Canada Junior Hockey League. He scored 51 goals each season. He led the league in assists with 117 one season and 86 the other. These are sensational statistics and he should have been the first choice of the pro teams in the summer of 1969 when he became eligible for the draft of graduating amateurs. But scouts knew of his diabetes and were afraid to take a chance on him.

Clarke tries—and fails—to sneak the puck past North Star goalie Cesare Maniago.

has heart, he is inspirational, he is a natural leader. Which was why I wanted him as captain." And general manager Keith Allen added, "I saw he was the one who took charge, not only on the ice, but in the dressing room. He has unusual quality as a person as well as outstanding talents as a player. He is the best team player I've ever seen."

Clarke never threatened to lead the league in goals because he often preferred to make a good pass which put a teammate in scoring position. He was especially good at winning face-offs, a critical skill because it put his team in possession of the puck. He handled the puck wonderfully well while skating and knew both how to make a perfect pass and how to receive one.

The Flyers were so tough they came to

be known as the Broad Street Bullies, and Bobby was as tough as any Flyer. Far from timid, he slashed, speared and hooked effectively with his stick. Those who met him off the ice found his on-the-ice aggressiveness surprising. He had an almost angelic face and was a shy and reserved young gentleman. In fact his quiet private life made him seem almost too good to be true.

In the rough and ready series between Team Canada and the Soviet National team in September 1972, Bobby helped turn the tide. The heavily favored Canadians had been surprised and embarrassed by the Russians through the first five games of the international test. Clarke saw that Valeri Kharlamov was running over Team Canada and so Clarke set out to teach him a lesson. He caught the Russian star with a sharp rap at the ankles, sending him right out of action. The Russians faded and the Canadians came on to win three straight games and the series.

"It's not something I was really proud of, but I hardly can say I was ashamed to do it," he admitted. The Soviet coach understood. Although he complained about the rough tactics of other NHL stars, he called Clarke the most valuable player on the other team.

Clarke then returned to NHL competition in the '72-73 season as captain of the Flyers. "I don't have many duties," he said. "The main one is to work hard and lead by example. But I'm not a holler guy. I don't go around slapping players on the back, calling team meetings or lecturing my teammates."

By the start of the '73-74 season, some were calling Clarke a millionaire as well as a superstar. He had signed with Philadelphia for only $14,000 a year in 1969. Three years later he signed a new five-year contract for $80,000 a year. Then, after his MVP season, he got a new seven-year contract that would pay more than $140,000 for each season of play. Instead of taking his whole salary at once, he agreed to take $50,000 a year for 21 years. "I don't think there are many 24-year-old guys who can say they've taken care of their family until 1994," he said proudly.

Yet for all the money and attention, Clarke had simple tastes. When Flyers' wives were asked to submit their husbands' favorite recipes for a story in the Flyers' program, Mrs. Clarke offered "Hot Dog Surprise"—a hot dog on a bun with mustard and relish. "Though I'm lucky enough to be making more money than the next guy, I'm very ordinary," he insisted. "I have a wife, a baby and a mortgage. I'm happy with my life. I'm doing what I most want to do."

One winter day Bobby learned that he was the favorite player of an 11-year-old boy who was dying in a nearby hospital. Bobby rushed to see him. As the boy talked to Bobby, he smiled and laughed for the first time in many days. Shortly afterward the boy lapsed into a coma and died.

"It's a scary sort of power to be able to brighten a little boy's last hours," Bobby said when asked about the visit. "It breaks your heart to see what he and his family were going through. They talk about my problem! He had one he couldn't lick. Mine is nothing. Mine I can live with. And live very well."

Yvan Cournoyer

The little fellow shot down the right side along the boards, then cut across toward center. He took a pass in full stride and kept the puck on the blade of his stick as he sped toward the goaltender. Suddenly he drew his stick back and with a short slapshot he drove the puck past the startled goalie.

This was in Moscow's Sports Palace in the eighth and final game in the series between Team Canada and the Russian National team. Each had won three games and tied one, and the winner of this game would win the series. Now little Yvan Cournoyer, star of the Montreal Canadiens, had tied the game for Canada —or thought he had. The red light signifying a score did not go on! The thousands of Canadians in the crowd began to boo. Alan Eagleson, the players' legal representative, was so angry he headed for the goal judge. He was stopped by Soviet police. Then the Canadian players stormed into the stands to protect him. And suddenly, an international incident seemed dangerously near.

When tempers cooled it turned out the light misfired, not Yvan Cournoyer. His goal counted, and a few minutes later, in the last minute of the game, Paul Henderson hammered home a rebound goal to win the game and the series. The 3,000 Canadians in Moscow and millions more watching on television in Canada went wild.

Cournoyer, a great favorite in French-speaking Canada, was one of the heroes. Called "The Roadrunner" after the cartoon character, he could appear as if by magic, strike and disappear again. *Beep-beep*, here he comes! *Beep-beep*, there he goes!

Later that year in National Hockey League competition, Cournoyer stole the puck from a Chicago defenseman, skated swiftly in on goaltender Gary Smith, and with a swift snap of his wrists drove the disk into the nets. It was the 250th goal of his major league career, a milestone attained in only nine years at the top.

Then in the Stanley Cup playoff finals in the last period of the last game, with the game tied, Cournoyer suddenly appeared in front of the Chicago Black Hawk goal. On a shot over the Chicago goal, the puck bounced off the glass backboard and right to Yvan. He darted in front of netminder Tony Esposito and swatted the puck into the net to win the Stanley Cup for Montreal.

Esposito said later, "He seemed to come from nowhere." Sportswriter Ben Olan commented, "It was as though a trap door had opened in the ice and the player had popped out of it."

The Roadrunner seemed to be here, there and everywhere. It was his 15th goal of the playoffs, the most any player had ever scored in one season's playoffs, and he was voted most valuable player in the post-season series.

Yvan Serge Cournoyer (pronounced *Coor-nwa-YAY*) was born November 22, 1943, in Drummondville, Quebec, 55 miles east of Montreal. "It is the dream

Playing for Team Canada, Yvan Cournoyer hugs teammate Phil Esposito after Phil scored.

Montreal's "Roadrunner" outraces Buffalo Sabre defenders down the ice.

of every French-speaking boy in Canada to become a player for Canadiens, no?" he said years later, his speech reflecting his French-Canadian background. It was his dream, but he seemed too small. So he spent his youth skating and skating because skating is the single most important skill in hockey, and is especially important to a little man.

When Yvan was growing up, his father ran a snow-machine parts shop in the Montreal suburb of Lachine. Since Yvan was interested in developing his shooting ability, he made himself a steel puck, which weighed three or four pounds, far more than the regulation puck, which weighs six ounces. He set up a target in the basement of his house and he shot the puck against it for hours at a time, bang, bang, until his mother nearly went crazy from the noise. When he went back to shooting a normal-weight puck, it felt like a feather. He could snap it off his stick, hard and accurately.

Yvan was signed into the Montreal system. In his last year as an amateur with the Montreal Junior Canadiens in the Ontario Hockey Association, he scored 53 goals and set up 63 others. Late in the season he was brought up for a trial with Montreal's major leaguers and was a sensation, scoring four goals in five games. Fans fell in love with him.

Like "Rocket" Richard, the legendary Canadien who retired in 1960, Cournoyer was a left-hander who was more comfortable on right wing. And he was an explosive scorer. But the resemblances ended there. Cournoyer was not nearly as big or powerful. At 5-foot-7 and 165 pounds, he could not dominate games as Richard could. In fact, at first, Canadien coach Toe Blake would not even play Cournoyer regularly.

The fans, always charmed by a promising little man, complained bitterly. *"On veut Cournoyer, on veut Cournoyer,"* they chanted—"We want Cournoyer, we want Cournoyer."

"I will use Cournoyer when I want to use him," Blake replied. "I will use him when we need a goal. He can play offense. He can't play defense. He can't check a damn."

Cournoyer was embarrassed when the fans called for him. But he was also resentful of Blake's attitude. Blake even sent him to the minors briefly. The experience "showed me for the first time I wasn't bound to be with the big team," Yvan recalled.

Beginning with the 1964-65 season, Cournoyer's first full season as a profes-sional, Blake used him primarily on the power play, when the other team was short-handed and did not have to be defensed determinedly. Yvan was a super power play specialist. But in his first four seasons he never scored as many as 30 goals a season because he did not play many regular shifts. Then in 1968 Blake retired and Claude Ruel took over. In his fifth season, Yvan finally broke through and scored 43 goals. But then in the play-offs he was benched again in favor of a defensive specialist. Yvan was disappointed once more, and the next season he fell into a slump.

Al MacNeil took over as coach during the 1970-71 season and Cournoyer took over a star role. The Roadrunner scored 37 goals in the regular season and 10 in the playoffs. The Canadiens won the Stanley Cup, but coach MacNeil was fired after the playoffs. Even a championship did not satisfy everyone in Montreal. The fans, the press and the management all seemed to expect perfection.

"All you can do is do your best to help the team win." Yvan said one night. "Life is too short to let the rest get to you," he shrugged.

In 1971-72, Cournoyer improved, scoring 47 goals, but the team, coached by Scotty Bowman, somehow let the title slip away. Then in '72-73 Yvan tallied 40 more times and added a record 15 goals in 17 playoff games as the Canadiens won their sixth championship in his nine years. In 1973-74 he hit 40 goals again.

At 30, he had come into his own. He had improved his defense. "It's a matter of effort," he said. "I can't move a big man around, but if I stay with him, I will bother him. I am not always drifting away looking for the interception or the break-away pass now."

Still, offense remained his strong suit. His greatest asset was his skating. His former center, Jean Beliveau, said, "The key to Yvan's skating is his start. He gets a quicker jump than anyone. He also can shift speeds and put on bursts which leave his defenders standing still. If they could, they would check him to death and drape themselves all over him to tie him up, as they tried to with 'The Rocket,' but they can't hit or stay with what they can't catch. Yvan is elusive."

Yvan explained how he had improved: "I have more control now. I do not skate ahead of myself. I give the puck a chance to catch up with me. I am a player who gets more breakaways than anyone, but

Cournoyer is in perfect scoring position—but the puck is between his legs.

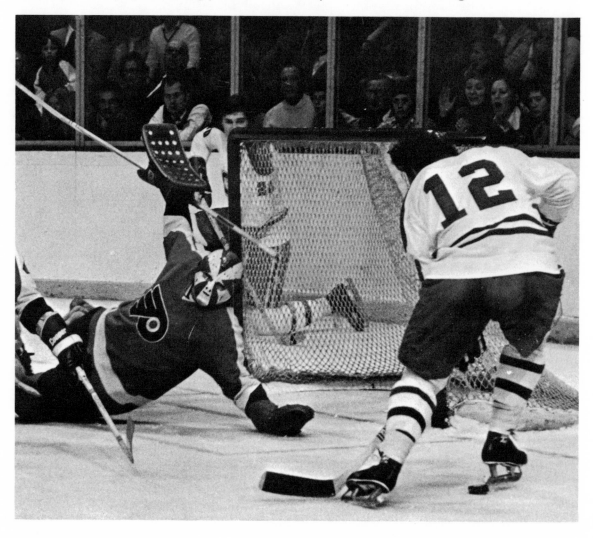

I have messed up more than anyone. I used to go too fast for control. Now I even put on fakes sometimes. What a pleasure it is to fake a goaltender on one shot and beat him with another! It is nice to be a smart player as well as a natural. But I am best being natural. Sometimes on breakaways I have too much time to plan. I am better on bang-bang plays."

But his shot also had a lot to do with Cournoyer's success. Opposing goalie Ed Giacomin, who had seen his share of Cournoyer goals go by, said, "He does not waste motion as do most shooters. He does not telegraph his delivery with a windup so you can get set. He is skating with the puck or he receives a pass and, whap, he has shot it. Many shoot harder, but few shoot so quick and with such accuracy from all angles. If you give him a hole, he'll find it."

As a little man, Yvan was picked on, especially in his first years in the league. He had to prove himself, even fighting bigger men. One summer he lifted weights to build himself up and took boxing lessons so he could better defend himself. "I don't want to fight, but I will fight if I have to," he said. "When players try to push me around, I push back. The more they push, the madder I get. The madder I get, the better I play. I wish I was bigger, but what can I do about that?"

Cournoyer's teammate, Jacques Lemaire, who was scarcely bigger than Yvan at 5-foot-10 and 170 pounds, summed up the problem of the little man: "We without the size make the most of what we have."

What about the future? Yvan took a philosophical view: "I do not set goals

Yvan takes on a bigger, stronger Bruin.

for myself because I do not want to worry myself sick about what I might have done. If I miss, I say I will do it next time. I do not want to worry about anything. I just want to play and enjoy the playing. There is pressure here enough without me putting more on myself. I have not started to slow down. I cannot afford to, because when your contributions to this club decrease, you are sent away. Here, you produce or you play for the ordinary teams other places."

Cournoyer was producing for an extraordinary team.

29

Ken Dryden

Ken Dryden explains to newsmen why he is "retiring" from the Canadiens.

A young man who enters professional sports may earn lots of money in a short time. Ken Dryden appeared as if by magic as goaltender for the Montreal Canadiens late in the 1970-71 season. The next year he earned $35,000 for the season, and played so well that he was given a new two-year contract for $70,000 a season. Again he lived up to his promise and earned his salary in 1972-73. But where was he in the fall of 1973 when the new season opened?

Dryden was in a law office working as a clerk for $7,500 a year. He declined to play the 1973-74 season for the Montreal Canadiens because they would not tear up his one-year-old contract for $70,000 a season and tender him a new one for five years at twice that amount. He in-

sisted it was not the money that mattered most, but the principle that counted.

A new hockey league, the World Hockey Association, had been formed, and suddenly salaries had gone up. Gerry Cheevers, formerly with the Boston Bruins, was earning $200,000 a year with the WHA's Cleveland Crusaders. And other goalies who had stayed in the NHL were making nearly as much.

"I didn't establish the going rate, I'm just asking to make it. It's my pride I'm thinking of as much as money," Dryden said after announcing his shift of employment. When his contract with Montreal ran out at the end of the 1973-74 season, hockey observers were betting that some team would offer Dryden "the going rate," and he would continue his sparkling career as one of the great young goalies and most interesting men in the game.

Kenneth Wayne Dryden was born in Islington, Ontario, on August 7, 1947. His mother was a schoolteacher, his father was a businessman and a frustrated athlete. Illness as a boy had prevented Mr. Dryden from pursuing sports, but he built his two sons hockey nets out of lumber and wire, and the neighborhood kids joined in games on the driveway rink. Later, when the Drydens moved into a bigger house, the father paved over the whole backyard as a rink.

Ken's older brother Dave also became a major league goaltender. The two brothers seemed naturally to favor playing in the nets. They used tennis balls instead of hockey pucks. "These were shot and bounced so fast, they sharpened my reflexes and developed my fast catching hand, which is my best asset," Ken said years later. "And tennis balls don't hurt when they hit you. When I started to play regular hockey in regular rinks the players couldn't shoot the puck hard enough to hurt you either. By the time I found out how much that hard rubber disk hurts when it hits you hard I was already grooved as a goaltender and it was too late to try another position."

The brothers were close and Dave dragged Ken after him and got him into games. So Ken kept playing with older boys while he was growing up, which matured and toughened him fast. From the age of seven Ken was playing organized hockey around Toronto. At 16, he was signed onto the Montreal Canadiens' negotiation list, but startled their master manager, Sam Pollock, by refusing to play junior where assigned, insisting on staying near home. Then when he finished high school he insisted on going to college instead of into hockey's minor leagues.

Some universities offered Ken scholarships to play basketball, but he settled for

In classic stand-up style, Dryden knocks the puck away with his stick.

a small scholarship to be educated at Cornell University in nearby New York State. He received tuition and books, plus $200 a year. He paid for his room and board by waiting on tables, washing dishes and doing other odd jobs. Summers, he did construction and demolition work as far away as Alaska. Meanwhile, he was the wonder of college hockey, permitting an average of fewer than two goals a game, losing only four games in three seasons and leading Cornell to the NCAA championship.

Ned Harkness, his coach at Cornell, recalled that Dryden was "bigger, quicker and much smarter than the average college player." College play was rapidly improving and was nearly as polished as play in Canada's junior amateur leagues, which developed most of the talent for the pro teams.

The Canadiens assumed Dryden finally was ready to turn pro after graduation from college, but he fooled them again. He wanted to go on to law school. Sam Pollock and his staff were amazed that Ken didn't jump at the chance to join the Canadiens. "I wanted to play hockey," Dryden recalled, "but I wanted to get my schooling, too. I felt that if I put it off to go into hockey I might never get back to it. I could see playing hockey for a living, but I couldn't see spending my life at it."

He finally took an offer to join the Canadian National Team on a three-year contract, with a scholarship to the University of Manitoba at Winnipeg. That way he could pursue his law studies and play hockey at the same time. However, after one year, the Canadian National Team collapsed. Since most of the really talented Canadian players were professionals, the National Team had trouble keeping up with teams from Russia, Czechoslovakia and other countries where top hockey stars played as amateurs.

Now Montreal's Pollock moved back into the picture with a contract offer to Ken that provided him a scholarship to McGill University so he could study law on the side. The Canadiens even agreed to let Dryden play only on weekends while he studied weekdays. Ken accepted and was assigned to the Canadiens' Montreal Voyageurs farm team.

This setup lasted less than one full season. Dryden was giving less than three goals a game in his first season with the Voyageurs. And Pollock was dissatisfied with his goaltenders on the Canadiens, who were struggling in third place in the NHL.

Late in the season, Pollock called Dryden up to the big team for a tryout. After watching three games, Ken was eased in with a start in Pittsburgh. "That is the only time I ever recall remaining nervous for a full game," he recalled. "My legs were shaking so bad I figured everyone in the arena knew it. I could hardly stand up. But somehow I made saves." He won the game.

The game that settled him down was one a few days later against the New York Rangers in Madison Square Garden before a capacity crowd of screaming Ranger rooters. He stopped 49 of 51 shots and won 6-2. "After that, I knew I could play in the big time," he said.

He returned to Montreal's Forum as the regular in goal. He gave up only nine scores in the six games he played before the regular season ran out.

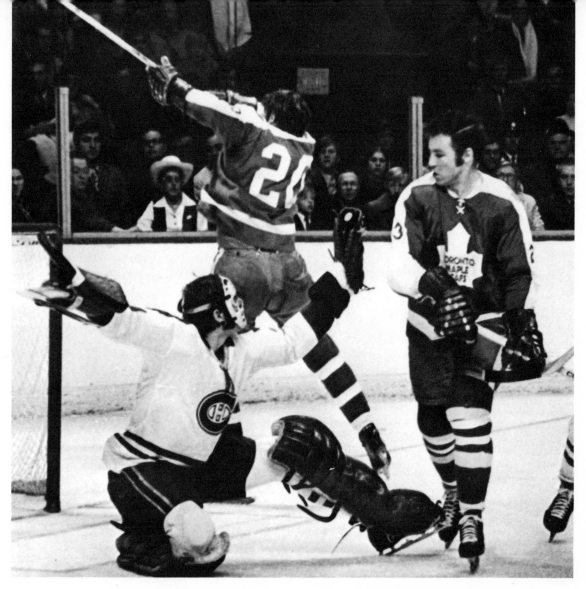

Ken makes a spectacular glove save against Toronto in his second NHL game.

Few figured Pollock would put the 23-year-old Dryden under the pressure of playoff competition, especially since he had so little NHL experience. But Pollock suggested that coach Al MacNeil give Ken a try. The experiment paid off. Dryden played every one of the 20 playoff games, setting a new league record with 1,221 minutes in goal. He opened in a seven-game upset of the big, bad Bruins from Boston, the regular-season leaders and the highest-scoring team in hockey history. At one point he shut them out for

90 minutes. Of course, other Canadiens were also important to the upset, but it was the giant, 6-foot-4, 210-pound goalie who surprised the Bruins.

Bruin veteran John McKenzie said, "Time after time we'd have him out of position and shoot at an empty net and I'd start to raise my stick to celebrate the score when—zap—that big mitt would come out of nowhere to catch the puck. That hand of his is something else."

The Canadiens went on to remove Minnesota in six games, then capped it all off with another seven-game victory over the Chicago Black Hawks.

According to statistics, there have been other more brilliant goaltending performances in playoffs. But circumstances conspired to make Dryden's showing seem really spectacular. He was young and unknown, he was handsome and well-spoken, and he had played a big part in the stunning upsets of the powerful Bruins and Black Hawks. He was voted Most Valuable Player of the playoffs. Overnight a hero was born.

He *was* good and he was going to get better. Despite studying as a full-time student, he found time to play 64 games for Montreal the following season. He had eight shutouts and a fine 2.24 goals-against average. Because he had played so few regular-season games the season before, he still was eligible for rookie of the year honors, and he won the award easily. The Canadiens lost in the playoffs, but Dryden's 2.83 mark was respectable. He was voted to the second All-Star team.

He stayed on top in 1972-73, playing 54 games despite a bad back, led the league with six shutouts and a 2.26 average, and won the Vezina Trophy as the league's most effective netminder. He helped his team to another Stanley Cup playoff triumph with a 2.89 average in 17 games, and was chosen to the first All-Star team. Then he "retired" and became a law clerk.

There are a number of ways to play goal. What counts is keeping the puck out of the net. But Dryden was especially admired because he had a classic style. He was a "stand-up" goaltender. He

A goalie's nightmare: Dryden is all alone as Phil Esposito (7) and Bobby Orr (4) drive in.

stayed erect and did not dive all over the ice to retrieve loose pucks. He blocked shots with his body, deflected them with his stick or kicked them away with his skates. But by catching most shots he controlled the puck, eliminating the rebounds which are frequently hammered right back at a goalie for a score. Unlike many netminders, he did not suffer from nerves and could play game after game without wanting relief. He was, above all, consistent.

Some hockey men distrusted Dryden because of his education. A *Sport* magazine cover poked gentle fun at him with a headline that read, "If Ken Dryden's So Smart, How Come He's a Goalie?" It seemed foolish to suggest that Dryden's education affected his performance on the ice, but it was true that he was quite different from the average pro player.

"I cannot let hockey make me what I am not," he told one reporter. "Hockey as a 24-hour-a-day, 365-day-a-year job is absurd. I am well aware there are other things in life. I love the law, among other interests.

"However, I also couldn't live with law alone. I find hockey fun and challenging. I don't see why I can't combine both for a while, at least. They said it would be impossible to be a full-time student and hockey player at the same time, but I didn't find it difficult. It kept my life interesting."

Dryden saw his hockey performance in a double way. It was intensely important to him, but when he first saw himself play on film, he was disappointed.

"I'd always thought of myself dipping and darting across the goal mouth with grace and everybody in the stands going 'ooh' and 'aah.' I was like a ballet dancer.

But on film I found out I was a dump truck, an elephant on wheels. I'm a 'stand-up' goalie because when I go down I'm too big to get up. I'm like a derailed train."

The constant attention of the fans sometimes disturbed him: "When they keep telling you you're the greatest and they know you're not and they're just trying to make an impression on you, pretty soon you're overwhelmed with the silliness of it and you just want to get away from it. These people mean well, but after a while they make you tired of yourself and your sport."

He found it difficult to live the life of a celebrity. After a game one night he told an interviewer he'd had a dozen interviews that week. The players started to tease him. They were nearly ready to leave, and they said, "Take your time, Dryden. You're the star and the bus can't go without you."

He grinned ruefully and hurriedly began to dress, apologizing to the interviewer. "I don't want the guys to get the wrong idea. Some of this attention embarrasses me."

As he rushed to finish dressing, he said, "A few big games in hockey hasn't made me a big man. I don't want to begin believing all that stuff they're saying or writing about me."

One of his teammates yelled, "Hey, Dryden, if you miss the bus tonight you'll be playing for Nova Scotia tomorrow."

He made the bus. But he missed the start of the season in 1973. It was not clear when or where he would play in goal again. But those who watched his great performances with Montreal suspect that the team offering him "the going rate" will get a bargain.

Phil Esposito

On March 11, 1971, Phil Esposito charged into the hockey record books. Already he had tied Bobby Hull's record of 58 goals in one season. Now in Los Angeles, where his Boston Bruins faced the weak Los Angeles Kings, he seemed certain to set a new standard.

There was little about his record in the newspapers and television reports in Southern California. The Kings' home arena, the Forum, was less than full as the game began, and there seemed to be no special excitement. In baseball when Roger Maris was challenging Babe Ruth's home run record the world waited impatiently for the news. But Los Angeles was new to big-time hockey and its fans either knew little or cared little about hockey records.

In the third minute of play, Esposito

Phil Esposito raises his stick in triumph after scoring his 59th goal of the season.

wristed a hard shot at the goal. But it clanged off the post and Phil's shoulders sagged. But five minutes later defenseman Ted Green passed the puck to Esposito, who was stationed in the "slot" about 15 feet to one side of the nets. The big center artfully angled his stick at the disk and deflected it past goaltender Denis DeJordy into the net.

The red light flashed and Phil's hands went high in the air. A wide smile illuminated his dark face, and his teammates, even those on the bench, came out to congratulate him.

Some L.A. fans applauded in polite appreciation and a small group of Bruin fans, who had paid $600 apiece to fly in from Boston, cheered and whistled. Then the announcer informed the unknowing what had just happened. About half of the crowd got to their feet to give him a standing ovation.

The Bruin rooters stood and waved their banners in the second period when Esposito scored his 60th goal. Together with his 67 assists, the goal gave him 127 points, surpassing his own 1969 record of 126. Then, as a small additional treat, Bobby Orr got a goal and an assist to break his previous records for scoring by a defenseman. The Kings' public address announcer kept the fans informed of each statistical milestone until Kings' general manager Larry Regan finally told him to stop. "The first one was all right, but what are we, publicity agents for these guys?" he growled.

The Bruins won easily. The Boston TV announcer then snatched Esposito from the grasp of the press for the post-game show. While the reporters waited, they talked to Orr, but it was clear they were waiting for Espo. When Phil finally

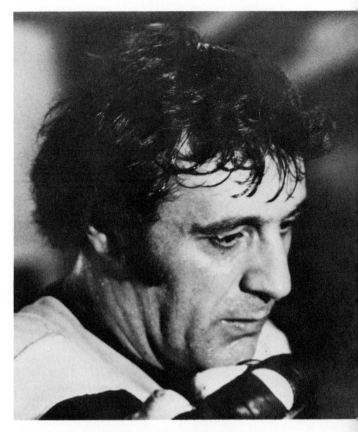

A few moments after his record-breaking goal, Phil takes a rest on the bench.

came in, the reporters ran from Orr, almost knocking over Bruin John McKenzie on the way.

"Tell 'em how great you are, Espo," McKenzie said jokingly.

Esposito laughed. A tough, good-natured man, he tried to tell everyone how good he was. But he was so modest and matter-of-fact that he seemed almost colorless. Offering no clever phrases, he gave credit to his teammates and tried to explain why he had said earlier in the season he could never break the scoring record.

He sat there in his long johns with perspiration soaking his long, curling, dark hair and running down his flushed, dark face. His nose was a little large for him to be called handsome, but he was ruggedly good-looking. And he seemed even larger than his 6-foot-1, 205 pounds. His big shoulders and big hands made him seem overpowering.

Someone asked how he felt about getting so many "garbage goals," scores on rebounds or deflections of other men's shots.

Sparks glinted from his eyes as he replied. "Stand in front and take the punishment you have to take there and you won't call 'em 'garbage goals.' Everyone's got a job to do. Mine is in front."

He stood up and stripped down. His body was covered with black and blue bruises, reddish welts and a small cut here and there. His foes slashed at him with their sticks and pounded him with their fists and bodies, but they couldn't push him away when he got into position in the slot or stop him from scoring.

As he headed for the shower, he put on an old, patched pair of shower thongs. "I can afford better," he admitted with a grin, "but I've had these since I joined Boston and I have my superstitions."

Espo seemed interested in everything from voodoo to fortune-tellers. Usually his interest was light-hearted, but he could fly into a rage at the sight of crossed sticks in a dressing room, considering them bad luck. "But I don't depend on luck," he said. "I work for what I get."

Most of the writers had left and all the other players had gone, so he showered alone. He came back and dried off and got dressed in his stylish clothes. The team bus had gone back to the Bruins' hotel without him, so he asked a few remaining writers for a lift to the hotel. As Jim Murray wrote, Roger Maris got a parade after his magic moment, but Phil Esposito had to bum a ride back to his hotel.

He held the two historic pucks which had been presented him that night and he said, "Me and Orr are going to pose together with our record pucks for picture plaques we can hang in our homes. Some considered me a one-season fluke, and I feel I've proven myself now. Inside, I'll have to admit, I feel very proud."

And then he walked out into the dark, cool night outside the arena. Even the autograph-seekers had given up and gone home.

He went on to score an astonishing 76 goals before the schedule ended, and assisted on 76 more, for a fantastic total of 152 points. The goals and the total points were two of hockey's most remarkable records. Expansion in the late 1960s had weakened the National Hockey League, diluting the talent, and a great player was often opposed by mediocre players. Espo's critics said that scoring was so much easier that his records didn't mean much. But if it was so easy, no other NHL stars had discovered the secret. Rocket Richard had set the first great scoring record by scoring 50 goals in 50 games, during World War II, when the war had taken many top players away and weakened defenses. By rights Esposito now ranked with the Rocket and Bobby Hull, "The Golden Jet," yet he had no glamorous nickname and remained curiously underrated.

Philip Anthony Esposito was born in Sault Ste. Marie, Ontario, February 2, 1942. His father built a rink in the backyard of their home and Phil practiced

Playing for Chicago in 1967, Phil scores against Bruin goalie Ed Johnston.

shooting against his brother Tony, who was one year younger. Phil went right into the Chicago Black Hawk organization from amateur ranks after scoring 32 goals for St. Catharines Teepees in the Ontario Hockey Association in the 1961-62 season.

Then in 1962-63, his first full season as a pro, Phil scored 36 goals and assisted on 54 for the old St. Louis Braves in the minor leagues. In February 1964 he was brought up to the Black Hawks. He was awkward and unsure of himself. He wasn't quite ready to be a star and scored only three times in 27 games.

But in the next three seasons he developed as a big, strong center to feed Bobby Hull, the Chicago star who was already

Espo wrestles with Ranger Jim Neilson in front of the New York goal in 1973.

breaking scoring records. Phil got the puck. And he got occasional goals himself by rebounding Bobby's blocked shots. Phil's scoring—between 20 and 30 goals a season—was nothing compared to Bobby's. Hull broke his own record with 54 goals in 1965-66 and got 52 the next season.

But Bobby seemed to be the only one who appreciated Phil, who was called a "garbage collector." It was said in Chicago that Esposito was too awkward and too slow and not eager enough to improve himself. He wasn't good defensively. He didn't seem to take the game or life seriously. When he was shut out in six games in the playoffs in 1967, the Black Hawk brass gave up on him.

Manager Tommy Ivan and coach Billy Reay were among the smartest of hockey men, but they made a mistake on Phil Esposito. They wanted a faster man to center for Hull. So in a trade with Boston, they got their fast center in Pit Martin, a muscular young defensive player in Gilles Marotte, and a journeyman goalie, Jack Norris. In exchange, the Bruins got three forwards—Esposito, Ken Hodge and Fred Stanfield. Some say that the Bruins pulled off the best trade—and the Black Hawks the worst—in hockey history. The three former Black Hawks became stars in Boston and after three seasons Boston had a Stanley Cup and new team scoring records.

When the deal was announced, a writer

40

asked Hull if he would miss Esposito. He said, "He was my right arm." Bobby never forgave the Hawks for trading Espo and five years later he jumped to the newly formed World Hockey Association.

Remembering the move to Boston, Espo said, "You hate to be traded. It's like you're a failure because your team doesn't want you any more. It's unsettling, but it's part of sports. You can be traded or sold or dropped at any time and you don't have any say. You play for the team that holds your contract or you don't play. You can't go to work for the company across the street the way a salesman can—unless a rival league springs up.

"But the trade was the best thing that ever happened to me. I got to Boston when I was developing into a good player just as the team there was developing into a good team. I got out of Hull's shadow and into Orr's shadow, which is the breaks. But the situation was different. I was able to become a leader up front, who was expected to shoot instead of pass."

In the next six seasons, Esposito went on a scoring spree like no one had ever seen before. He set NHL records with 77 assists and 126 points in the 1968-69 season, then set records with those 76 goals and 152 points two seasons later. The next two years he topped 130 points, making him the unchallenged leader in goals and total points.

In the 1973 Stanley Cup playoffs, Espo seriously injured his knee. Through the summer and fall, fans wondered if the injury would slow him down. But he recovered quickly from an operation, and in his first regular-season game he scored a hat trick—3 goals. He had 20 goals in the first 18 games, the fastest any player ever has scored that many. He disproved his doubters in a hurry.

By season's end he had put together startling league-leading totals once again —68 goals and 77 assists for 145 points. And the Bruins had the best won-lost record in the league.

Led by Esposito and Orr, the Bruins had moved up from third in 1967-68, to three first-place and three second-place finishes in the next six years. But of course the real test was in the playoffs for the Cup.

His first playoff in Boston, Esposito was blanked in four games and Montreal knocked the Bruins out in four straight. In 1969 he got eight goals and 10 assists in 10 games. But he blew big chances in the last two games as Boston was eliminated by Montreal again.

But by 1970 the Bruins were ready. Espo led the way with 13 goals and 14 assists, setting records for goals and points in the playoffs. The Bruins won the championship for the first time in 30 years. In the semi-finals, Phil had scored a hat trick in the first game and five goals in four games off his brother Tony, who was now the star goalie for Chicago.

The brothers were close off the ice. But Phil said, "On the ice, it is as if he was not my brother. On the ice I would score against my mother if I could."

The Bruins lost in the 1971 playoffs. Then, just before the start of the regular season in the fall of 1972 Phil captained Team Canada past Russia in that celebrated international series. Bobby Orr was out with an injury, and Bobby Hull could not play because he had jumped to the WHA. So Espo was the one big gun left. He came through by leading all scorers with seven goals and eight assists in eight games. In the final game, Russia led by two goals going into the last period. Esposito scored his second goal of the game swiftly to bring Canada close. Then he passed to Yvan Cournoyer for the tying goal. And in the last minute Phil dug out the puck and smashed a hard drive that the goalie couldn't handle.

The puck bounced out to Paul Henderson, and he knocked in the big winning goal. Back home, all Canada went wild. "I guess I finally got some recognition," Phil laughed later.

In 1972-73 Phil continued his heroics. The Bruins finished second to Montreal in the regular season, but in the playoffs Espo scored nine goals and 15 assists as the Bruins blasted to another Stanley Cup triumph.

Phil had led all scorers in the NHL five years out of six and set amazing new records doing it. But he was voted Most Valuable Player only once, in 1969. Some of his fans were angry about this lack of recognition, but Phil took it in stride.

He viewed himself as a workman. "My biggest asset is my size and strength," he said. "I can reach over a guy and still get off a shot. I go where I want to go, and when I'm where I want to be I'm hard to budge.

"I do a job. I do it without a lot of style. Orr has the magnetism. Hull is explosive. I'm a workman. I'm just Esposito, never a crowd-pleaser. Hey, I've watched myself on videotape and I wouldn't cheer for me, either. But that's me. I just don't look good doing what I do, but I do it good. A guy does what he does best, whatever he does. A guy digs the best ditch he can."

Phil Esposito digs some ditch.

Tony Esposito

Tony Esposito slams a shot away from the Chicago goal with his stick.

"Goaltending is a job," Tony Esposito once said. "It's a tough, dangerous job. There is pressure every time you are in there. It was torture for me when I was a kid and it's still torture for me whenever the puck goes in. Not doing your job scares you. The older you get, the more afraid you get.

"To be playing well as a goalkeeper you have to be afraid. Not petrified, exactly, but you have to be afraid. Not afraid that you'll get hurt, but afraid

they're going to score on you. Every time they come down the ice with that puck, I'm afraid the puck is going to go in. If it goes in, you get blamed. If it goes in too often, your team gets beat and you get blamed.

"In practice, I'm physically afraid I'm going to get hurt. I back up. I try to get out of the way. In practice, you don't have the adrenalin going for you like you do in a game.

"Who the hell likes to have pucks shot

at them at a hundred miles an hour from 15 or 20 feet? I tell them in practice, take it easy, don't blast away. But they do, they crank up from ten or 15 feet out. If that puck goes into that mask at 120 miles an hour, it will ring your bell, all right. A concussion maybe. The mask keeps it from splitting your face open. But there's still places exposed on your head you can get cut. And having the mask banged against your face by a puck can break your bones.

"But in games, I'm only afraid of being scored on. I don't back up. I forget the fear of getting hurt. I push it out of my mind. It's the giving up the goals, the getting beat that bothers me. It's being blamed that bothers me. It's a job and it pays good, so I do it. But I don't like it. No, I don't like it. I do it because I can make a good living at it."

Like his brother Tony, Phil Esposito called playing hockey a job. But for Phil it was fun. He was out front, getting goals, setting up goals, winning scoring championships. His game was scoring goals. But for Tony, the All-Star goaltender of the Chicago Black Hawks, the game was trying not to give up goals and worrying about being scored on. Offense is the glamour game. Defense is negative. A great save is one of the most spectacular plays in the sport, but it is swiftly forgotten. It is the winning goal that is remembered.

For brother Tony Esposito, hockey really was a job, and it wasn't fun. Tony was different from his brother both in appearance and personality. He was shorter, stockier, rounder of face. He was a worrier, who brooded about his job and found life difficult. Both brothers were tough,

but Tony was the one who faced fear in every game and would not give in to it.

James Anthony Esposito was born April 23, 1943, in Sault Ste. Marie, Ontario, just across the border from Northern Michigan. He and Phil shared Anthony as their middle names, but Philip Anthony became "Phil" and James Anthony became "Tony." No one remembers why. Tony was a little more than a year younger than Phil.

They grew up talking and thinking hockey. They used to play one of those

Playing for the Canadiens, Tony stops a shot by his brother Phil (7) of Chicago.

table-top hockey games played by kids all over Canada. Phil recalled, "I'd pull the lever and slap the steel marble all over the place, and even then Tony used to make some terrific saves."

Their father made nets for their driveway, then refinished the family basement into a long recreation room. Indoors, the boys strapped pads on their legs, dropped to their knees and played a kind of hockey by slapping a rolled-up stocking along the floor with their hands.

They often got up at four or five in the morning, loaded Tony's goalkeeping gear on a toboggan and dragged it to the nearest outdoor rink to play all day long. They played by themselves until others showed up. In baseball all kids want to bat, and in hockey all kids want to shoot. Since Phil was the oldest he got to shoot, and Tony had to play goalie, trying to stop the shots. He got so good that when teams were formed everyone wanted Tony to be the goalie. He didn't like it at first, but he liked being wanted. His father, fearful Tony would get hurt, begged him to play another position, but Tony stubbornly insisted he wanted to stay in the nets.

Even then Tony learned that the goalie is often blamed for defeats. In one city tournament game he gave up goals on two long shots and his team lost. Phil cursed his brother until Tony began to cry. Mr. Esposito had Tony's eyesight checked and he was found to be nearsighted, so he got eyeglasses and he improved overnight. In a later city tournament game he made 77 saves and he was voted most valuable player in the tourney. Phil was voted most likely to succeed in the same series. The brothers were together off and on the ice, but ex-tremely competitive. Phil recalled, "I got into many a fight for Tony and he got into many a one for me. But we also had some groovy fights with each other. Once I knocked a hole right through our basement wall when we were fighting. My father never found out. We covered the hole with a picture of Jesus."

"Tony was always a worry wart, a very, very nervous boy," his father remembered years later. "Phil took a loss better. He forgot about it."

Tony agreed: "I couldn't forget a loss, or even a bad game. Even in the bantams, Phil and the other kids would moan and complain when a puck got by me. The pressure got to me. I couldn't stop worrying."

When he was in high school, Tony quit the game for a year. There was no junior team in their hometown. Phil had quit school to play for a junior team in St. Catharines, 200 miles away. But Tony stayed in school and played football instead. But then a junior hockey team was organized in town and Tony was asked to try out for it. So he gave the game another chance and became the team's regular goalie.

More studious than his brother, and less eager to turn pro, Tony accepted a hockey scholarship to Michigan Tech in nearby Houghton, Michigan. Michigan Tech is nowhere by American football standards, but it was strong in hockey. Tony took a degree in business administration, and helped the Michigan Tech hockey team win the NCAA championship. He allowed fewer than three goals per game and received honorable mention for All-America.

After graduation, he signed with the

Montreal Canadiens. He turned pro during the 1967-68 season at the advanced age of 24 and had a fair year for Vancouver's minor league team. Montreal moved him to its minor team in Houston and he went well for the first half of the 1968-69 season, then was called up to complete the campaign with the Canadiens. In 13 games, he held foes to fewer than three goals a game and scored two shutouts. However, the Canadiens were dissatisfied with him.

There are purists in hockey who feel style is essential, and Tony was not a stylish goalie. He was a "fall-down" goalie who flopped all over the ice, diving this way and that to make saves. He often seemed to be out of position. But

Tony puts on a rare smile for the camera.

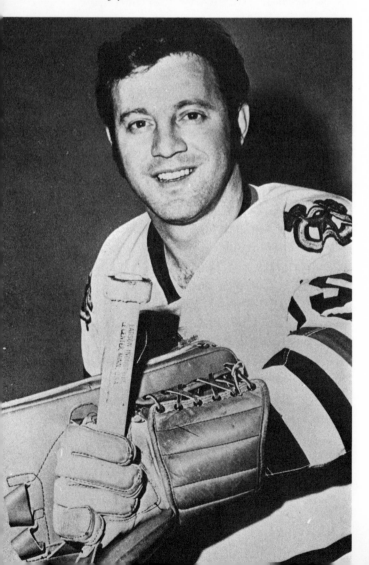

his great reflexes and extremely fast hands and feet allowed him to make the saves anyway. But the Canadiens were not convinced. They failed to protect Tony in the 1969 intra-league draft, and he was snapped up by the Black Hawks.

"You do it any way you can do it," Tony said in defense of his play. "It doesn't matter how you do it, just so you do it. The Canadiens had so much talent up there they didn't give a guy much of a chance to prove himself. They always figured they had one coming up who was better. I'm glad they let me go. They had so many goalkeepers I was afraid I wouldn't get to play much. And if you don't play you can't improve and you can't make the pay. I didn't like the way the coach, Claude Ruel, handled goaltenders. If you let in a bad goal, he'd give you hell. He got me to pressing. I can't be handled like that. I worry enough all on my own. I need encouragement."

The Black Hawks wanted Tony as a backup for their regular goalie Denis DeJordy. But Tony performed so well that they soon traded DeJordy and gave the job to Tony. Chicago coach Billy Reay said, "Tony fooled us. We got him because we thought he might become good. It turned out he already was great. He may not look like much, but he's a lot of goaltender. I don't care if he plays on his ear, he keeps the puck out, which is what counts."

Bobby Orr agreed. "He looks like hell," he once remarked. "He does everything wrong. He gives the shooters all sorts of openings. He doesn't play the angles properly. He doesn't even keep his legs together. He gives you holes half the net wide. But when you shoot for them, he closes them up. You think you've got him,

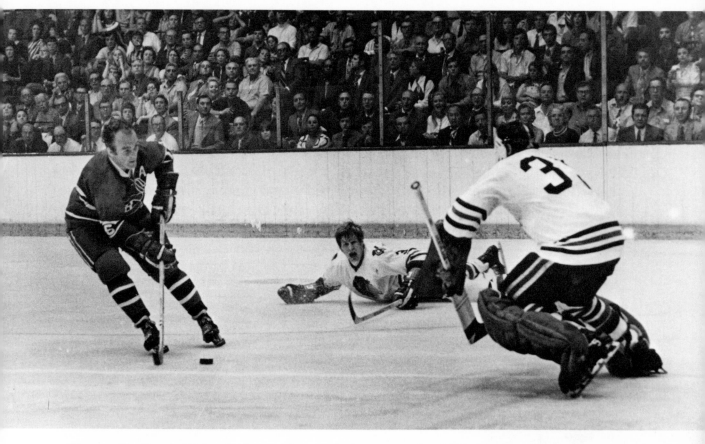

Montreal's Henri Richard shoots the goal that won the 1971 Stanley Cup against a helpless Tony Esposito. Keith Magnuson (center) wasn't able to assist on defense.

then he's got the puck. He's amazingly quick. He has to work harder than smooth goalies. But he gets the job done."

Tony was a sensation his first full season in the majors. He set a modern record with 15 shutouts. It is not hard to hold foes to two or three goals a game if you are one of the great ones, but it is hard to hold them without a goal for 15 games no matter how great you are. It was one of those seasons. His goals-against average was 2.17, which won the Vezina Trophy for the most effective record in the nets. He also was voted rookie of the year.

Tony came back the next season to record a 2.27 mark with six shutouts. Then in 1971-72 he averaged only 1.76, winning another Vezina with his back-up goalie Gary Smith under revised rules which give the prize to the team with the lowest goals-against average. Tony also piled up nine more shutouts.

In the 1972-73 season, Tony went 2.51 with four shutouts. "The team was weaker so my record was worse," Tony explained. "A goalie is at the mercy of his teammates to some extent. I don't blame my teammates for the goals I give up. We all share in it. We're a team. We all have our jobs to do."

Nevertheless, goalies still get blamed for defeats much more than do other players, and Tony was blamed for the Black Hawks' failure to take the Stanley Cup. In 1970, he was riddled by 27 goals in eight games, an average of more than three a game. He gave up a hat trick and five goals in four games to his brother Phil as Boston eliminated the Black Hawks in four straight.

In 1971 he bounced back with a splendid 2.19 mark in 18 games. The Hawks went to the seventh game of the finals against Montreal, and Tony was shutting out the Canadiens 2-0 late in the second period when Jacques Lemaire lofted a high, easy shot from mid-ice. Somehow it escaped Esposito and bounced into the nets. The Canadiens gained heart and attacked relentlessly in the last period. Henri Richard put two shots past Esposito to win the game and the Cup for Montreal.

"It was a long time before I recovered from that one," Tony said wistfully. "But I played a good game. Everyone had to see that. We should have won. But I let one bad one get by. So I was blamed."

In 1972 the Black Hawks were eliminated from the playoffs in five games. Then in 1973 Tony helped carry the Hawks to the seventh game of the finals against Montreal. The Hawks lost again, as Tony gave up six goals. It was a badly played series, a defenseless series, in which both goaltenders were riddled almost to the point of shell-shock. Montreal's Ken Dryden said, "Play was loose and we both suffered and struggled all the way. It wasn't a goaltender's series."

Although many clubs had begun to use two goaltenders equally, giving each about 40 games, Tony Esposito continued to play close to 60 games a season. The Hawks traded away his back-up goalie going into 1973-74, figuring Esposito could carry the load consistently. He did, playing in 70 games, winning 34, recording ten shutouts and posting a goals-against average of just over two a game.

Early that season, after scoring the 40th shutout of his five-year career, the 30-year-old veteran sat wearily in front of his locker, resting before he could get out of his gear. He said, "The thing that wears you out is the worry. I'm not as bad as I used to be, but giving up goals still bothers me and losing games still bothers me. It takes me two or three hours to unwind after any game. I'm very nervous going in and very nervous after it's all over.

"People wonder why I don't laugh more, like Phil. Well, Phil's not a goaltender. I don't find anything funny in playing goal. But I don't know anything I could do besides playing goal that would make me anywhere near the kind of money I'm making. So I play goal. I'm hard on my family all season and I try to make it up to them between seasons.

"It's not an easy life. I've learned I'm going to be blamed for every goal I give up. I don't like it. But I've learned to live with it."

Off in a corner, coach Billy Reay was talking about a goal the Hawks had given up in Vancouver. Someone pointed out to him it was the only goal Tony had given up in three games. Smiling, Billy said, "Yeh, but it was a bad goal. It never should have been scored. Of course, I don't blame Tony, mind you."

Of course. Tony wasn't laughing.

Rod Gilbert

New York's Rod Gilbert waits for a rebound from the Canadien goalie.

Rodrique Gabriel Gilbert was visiting his hometown. The New York Ranger star arrived in Montreal the day before a game with the Montreal Canadiens and visited his family in the suburb of Point Aux Trembles. In Point Aux Trembles, as in much of Montreal, only French is spoken. Gilbert (pronounced *Jeel-BEAR*) grew up in a red brick house on the Rue St. Jean Baptiste. As a boy, he practiced shooting by slapping a puck against the side of the house and chipping away the bricks. And when his parents gave him his first hockey skates, he took them to bed with him the first night.

Gilbert visited the school across the street, Roussin Academy, where he and Joseph Gilbert Yvon Jean Ratelle—his teammate on the Rangers—had studied a little and played a lot of hockey. English was taught as a foreign language here. Some in the neighborhood advocated an independent French nation in Eastern Canada. And nearly everyone considered hockey the one great sport. Many of Gilbert's friends never forgave him for signing with the Rangers instead of the hometown Canadiens, hockey's most rabidly supported team.

Now it was February 1968. Rod Gilbert was in his seventh season with the Rangers. After visiting his family, he joined the team at the Sheraton Mont Royal Hotel. He slept until nine in the morning. He had breakfast with Ratelle and other teammates at ten. He walked around downtown, then lounged in the hotel lobby awhile, reading the French and English language newspaper sports sections. He had a steak with the team at lunch at two in the afternoon, then returned to his room and took a nap. Finally it was time to go to the Forum, Montreal's famous sports arena, home of the Canadiens. Gilbert took a cab down St. Catherine Street West to the Forum. In the dressing room, he put on his red, white and blue uniform, bulky with the many hard pads that made him look bigger than his 5-foot-9, 175-pound frame really was.

The arena was packed. Every Canadien game for years had been sold out—fathers passed precious season tickets to sons in their wills. Here, visitors could be made to feel like intruders. Although the program and public-address announcements were in French and English, the fans cheered on their team in French. Perhaps Gilbert's family and friends were rooting for him, but the other thousands were passionately for the Canadiens. Little did they know that this game would be Gilbert's.

Early in the first period, he shot with his wrists from five feet out for a goal.

In the second period, he and Ratelle got loose on a breakaway and Ratelle fed him a pass. Gilbert slapped it past the goalie. Later in the same period he unleashed a slapshot from 50 feet out that fooled the goalie, giving Rod a "hat trick." But he wasn't finished. Early in the third period, he backhanded a Ratelle rebound into the cords for his fourth goal of the game.

The Rangers won 6-1, a rare victory for a visiting team at the Forum. After the game, Gilbert was all smiles, proud to have put on such a show in his hometown. But he was modest about the four goals. "I had 16 shots tonight and any night you have 16 shots you may get four goals," he said. "A lot of this game is luck and a lot of it is being in the right place at the right time. There are nights you don't get any shots so you can't get any goals, and there are nights you get the puck but the other players are in the best spots to shoot, so the best play is to pass. Tonight, it was just my night. There are worse nights ahead."

He was right, of course. That was one of the high points of his career, during which he has been up and down many times. One of Rod's early coaches was Yvan Prud'Homme, a scout for the Rangers. He got the young player to agree reluctantly that he had a better chance of making the Rangers, then a second-rate team, than his beloved, all-conquering Canadiens. Rod suggested that his friend Jean Ratelle be signed, too, and Prud'Homme reluctantly agreed. Ratelle became a top performer for the Rangers, although he was less spectacular than Rod.

At 15, Gilbert had gone to Guelph in

the English-speaking province of Ontario to play Junior A amateur hockey. Almost everyone he knew there—teammates, residents of his boarding house, even shopkeepers—spoke English. He was lonely and homesick for a long time. But within a year he had learned to speak English.

In 1961, in what was to be his last game as an amateur, he tripped on the lid of a cardboard ice cream container which an unthinking fan had thrown on the ice, and crashed into the sideboards, cracking his spine. He was sent to the Mayo Clinic in Minnesota, sitting up 20 hours on the train because it hurt too much to lie down. There, doctors did a "spinal fusion," grafting a piece of bone from his leg to join the part in the spine.

Neither the spine nor the leg healed well. A blood infection developed in his leg which was so bad that doctors thought they'd have to amputate. Gilbert

did mend, however, and played his first games for the Rangers in the 1962 Stanley Cup playoffs.

Then in the summer of 1965, when he was lifting something heavy his spine parted again. This time, the Ranger team doctor operated, performing a second spinal fusion. For weeks, Rod lay in St. Clare's Hospital across from Madison Square Garden doubting he'd ever play again. "It was the worst time of my life," he said later. "Ever since I returned to action I've lived in dread of hurting my back again. I couldn't take a third operation. I just couldn't."

He played after that in a back brace or a corset, both of which limited his movements but protected his back. He played in almost constant pain and had to prove to opponents that he was still tough and willing enough to fight if pushed around. Like other players, he suffered a host of other lesser injuries.

Vic Hadfield congratulates Gilbert on a goal as two Maple Leafs look for the puck.

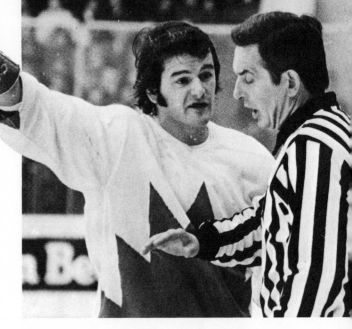

Rod complains about a referee's call.

His handsome face showed faint traces of more than 200 stitches. Yet he points out with pride, "The back injuries knocked me out, but I was out only one period from all the other cuts and stitches."

A quick, clever skater and an explosive shooter, he averaged 26 goals and 40 assists per season through his ten full campaigns in New York. A good outside shooter, perhaps too eager for slapshots from long range, he became an expert with the extremely curved "banana" blade in the late 1960s. His shots dipped and fluttered like knuckle-balls, and he intimidated goalies. When the league later passed new rules, virtually outlawing the hooked sticks, however, Gilbert adjusted. He improved his inside wrist shots, improved at making and receiving passes, and shot fewer of his long slapshots.

Despite his fine record, Gilbert was often a villain to Ranger fans. For one thing, he never lived up to the buildup he got when he broke in. He had scored 54 goals in 47 games in his last season as a junior. He arrived in New York at the start of the 1962 Stanley Cup playoffs. In his first game he set up a goal against Toronto and in the fourth game he scored his first two goals.

Then came the letdown. He scored only 11 goals his first full season. Five of his next six years he scored more than 24 goals, but when he scored only 16 in 1969-70, his eighth season, he was booed in Madison Square Garden. Fans said he was a playboy and complained that he was not willing to sacrifice his personal pleasures for success. And they blamed him for the Rangers' failure year after year to win the Stanley Cup.

Two years later, Gilbert and his teammates seemed destined to be champs. In 1971-72, he tallied 42 times. With Ratelle (46 goals) and Hadfield (50 goals), Rod made up the G-A-G (Goal-a-Game) Line, the second-highest scoring line in NHL history.

In the 1972 Stanley Cup playoffs, Gilbert gave a heroic performance. In the semi-finals against the Black Hawks, he darted in on the brilliant goaler Tony Esposito during power plays and ripped low, wicked shots past him to decide the second and fourth games.

In the finals against the Bruins, he was an inspirational leader. Boston was burying the visiting Rangers, 5-1, midway in the first game, and the Boston fans were hooting the troubled visitors. Then Gilbert took a pass, accelerated past one defenseman, shifted past another, and drove a hard shot through a small hole allowed by goalie Gerry Cheevers. This ignited a Ranger surge that tied the game, 5-5. His passes set up two scores in the comeback. The Bruins won the game with a late score, but Ranger confidence had been revived.

In the second game, with Boston leading early in the middle period, Ranger defenseman Jim Neilson stole the puck and fed Rod a perfect lead pass. He flashed in on Boston goalie Ed Johnston and jammed a short, high shot past him to tie the game. Again, however, the Bruins won with a late goal.

In New York for the third game, late in the first period, Gilbert took a pass from Brad Park, made a move that sent goalie Cheevers sprawling, and flipped the puck past him to bust open a tight contest and send the Rangers on to their first triumph of the series. Boston was too strong and finally overwhelmed the Rangers, but Gilbert had proved himself as a pressure performer.

That summer the Ranger stars were signed to lavish, long-term contracts to protect them from a raid by the new World Hockey Association. Gilbert drew the second highest salary—$175,000 a season for three years. The '72-73 season was another Ranger disappointment, and Rod scored only 25 goals. But early in the 1973-74 season he scored his 273rd goal and later his 730th point to surpass Andy Bathgate's all-time Ranger records. He finished the season with 36 goals and 41 assists for 77 points.

"I'm not a Bobby Hull or a Bobby Orr, who can skate around people or over people, who can take the puck and go all the way with it, who doesn't need anyone else," Rod said, evaluating his play. "I need linemates and teammates who complement my style and help me, who get me the puck. I'm a good player, but I'm not as spectacular as people expect me to be.

"I have big games and I have big years. But I have games and I have years when the puck doesn't bounce right for me. I can't win pennants and playoffs by myself. I'm a professional and I do the best I can. I'm sorry if the people are disappointed."

Emile "Cat" Francis, who guided Gilbert throughout his Ranger career, said, "He is one of the guttiest guys I've ever known, and one of the greatest players. He has overcome great obstacles and a lot of pain to become good. He's a serious player. If anything, he worries too much to play relaxed. Which is why he has slumps."

Gilbert sighed and admitted, "I am a worrier. I am a pessimist. It makes me a streaky player. If I get going good, I gain confidence and feel nothing can stop me. If I start going bad, if I hit a few goalposts with shots or the goalies make some great saves on me, I start to lose confidence in my shot and start to pass more.

"Maybe that's why I live loose off the ice. I feel tight on the ice. Maybe it's the fear of further injury. I force myself to forget it, but it's always there in the back of my mind."

If Rod was not always a hero among hockey fans, he cut a fine figure in New York's stylish night life. He dressed elegantly, drove expensive cars, and often escorted beautiful women to movie openings and night clubs. Thinking about his two lives, off and on the ice, he said with a slight smile, "It is a soft life, maybe, but a hard game."

Bill Goldsworthy

Goldsworthy skates onto the ice wearing the helmet that helped make him a success.

In his first full NHL season in 1967-68, Bill Goldsworthy played for the Minnesota North Stars, one of six brand new expansion teams. He scored only 14 goals in 68 games. However, in the playoffs he exploded with eight goals and 15 scoring points in only 14 games to lead all players in those categories in post-season play.

The following season, he started so slowly and played so listlessly that he was unceremoniously sent back to the minor leagues. There he raged to four goals in six games and was hurriedly restored to the majors. He finished the season with only 14 goals again. Minnesota did not even make the playoffs.

Then in 1969-70, Goldsworthy went on a tear and tallied 20 goals by midseason, finished up with 36, and added four more in only six games in the playoffs. "He is," said his Minnesota manager and coach Wren Blair, "a most unpredictable young person and player. He has talent he hasn't used yet and sometimes needs a kick in the pants to bring it up."

Explaining his erratic tendencies, the tall, blond Goldsworthy said, "I had no confidence my first season in the majors, but the puck bounced right for me in the playoffs at season's end and after that I felt I had the club made. You're scared all the time of not making it and when you make it you become cocky. You hustle to make a place for yourself in the majors and when you make it you naturally let down.

"I didn't give it an all-out effort my second season. I don't mean I wasn't trying. I was. No one ever deliberately dogs it. But I didn't have that little extra desire I'd had my first year. I figured the goals would come. When things went wrong I got disgusted and said the hell with it.

"When I was sent down, I was really disgusted. I figured after the playoffs I'd had I deserved more time to get going. I figured the club was making a mistake and had misjudged me. But it shook me up. I mean, after you've been in the majors, the minors is no place to be. Fortunately, I was determined to beat my way back up to show my bosses how wrong they were. They did bring me back up, but I still didn't set the world on fire. I was trying too hard. A player plays best relaxed, confident. When he's struggling, when he starts to press, he takes shots too soon or too late, he shoots when he should pass, he passes when he should shoot, he thinks too much. A player shouldn't think too much.

"But I had learned a lesson. I came to camp the next season in the best shape of my life. I had conditioned myself during the off-season. I was ready to play from the first exhibition game. The more you play, the sharper you get. I was hustling hard. Looking back on it now I can see I had a lot to learn. I wasn't giving as much as I thought I was. I can see now you can always give more. The thing is, we're not all the same inside. To some, hustle is a way of life. They try to run through brick walls if necessary to get where they want to be. To others, having fun is the most important part of life and work is secondary. We all want to do well at what we do, but some are willing to go harder at it.

"I'm one of those guys who has to psych myself up to give the extra effort that pays off. Some guys like me never

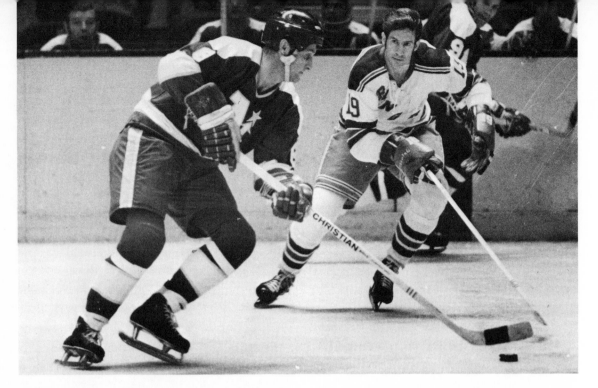

With the puck on his stick, Bill Goldsworthy races past Ranger Jean Ratelle.

make it. There are a lot of guys with the ability of superstars who never make it because they just aren't willing to make the sacrifices. I'm not saying they're wrong—we all want different things out of life. I want to enjoy life, but I also want to be a superstar enough to push myself to it."

After such careful preparation, Bill scored only six goals in the first half of the '69-70 season. He clearly considered the campaign a loss, and was down in the dumps again. Contemplating the second half, he observed, "I've got two chances to make something of this season—slim and none."

Then one day in practice he collided with teammate Jean-Paul Parise and suffered a brain concussion. Doctors advised him to wear a helmet to protect his head. Suddenly, the newly helmeted Bill Goldsworthy set out on a scoring spree seldom equaled in pro hockey.

He scored goals in six straight games,

missed one, then scored in seven more in succession. This gave him 13 out of 14. After being stopped another game, he scored in ten of his next eleven games, giving him goals in 23 of 26 games. He scored three goals in one game in Los Angeles, then four the next game in Vancouver, giving him seven goals in two games in two nights.

Jean-Paul Parise suggested he should get paid for giving Goldsworthy the concussion. Bill's wife said, "Maybe every time he's going bad somebody should give him a hit in the head."

Bill, himself, shrugged and smiled, "I guess I'm sort of streaky by nature. I just got hot." He decided to keep the helmet for good. "It's hot," he said, "but it makes me hot. It may make me braver."

A few years earlier, no self-respecting hockey player would have been caught on the ice wearing a helmet. But they seemed to be slowly catching on. Another North Star, Bill Masterson, had died of a skull fracture in 1968 when he hit his head on the sideboards. Some fans suggested that helmets be required by the league. But many players considered a helmet the mark of a coward. And fans, who enjoy being able to recognize their favorite players on the ice, complained that helmets would make recognition more difficult.

But Goldsworthy, his prematurely thinning hair concealed by a helmet, proved that a player with a helmet could become a scoring star. He became the big attraction of the new Minnesota team, winding up with 34 goals that season and scoring 31 the next. Then in 1973-74, big Bill banged in 46 goals. After seven seasons in the big time Bill had established himself as a big player, something of a showboat, who went into a victory dance, called "The Goldie Shuffle," every time he got a goal.

William Alfred Goldsworthy was born August 24, 1944, in Kitchener, a city of 125,000 persons in southern Ontario. His father had been a semi-pro baseball pitcher and hockey player. Bill was skating on outdoor rinks at five and playing organized leagues at seven, wearing rolled up magazines under his stockings as shin-guards. He lost his front teeth to a hockey stick at 12. And he was even tougher off the ice, running with a group called "The Falcons," who fought gang wars in gravel pits. Bill was arrested once for taking some records from a music store, but he was let off with a warning. "Sports saved me from a life of crime," he once said with a smile, only half-kidding.

Goldsworthy also played football and

later remembered, "I loved to hit. I just liked to come—bang—and just crucify guys. I liked contact. I was that way off the field. If I thought someone had taken my bike, I'd beat him up first, then ask about the bike. And on the ice I was a hitter before I could skate with any speed or shoot worth a darn."

His family lacked a refrigerator, so every Saturday night Bill's dad would send him to the store for cold soda pop and they'd sit in front of their small TV set sipping soda, munching popcorn and watching "Hockey Night in Canada," the weekly televised NHL game.

Bill saw hockey as a way out of what he called a "lunch bucket life." He was signed by Boston and at 18 sent to Niagara Falls to play Junior A for $22.50 a week, plus room and board. A teammate there was Derek Sanderson, who became a Boston Bruin star and rebel. The Junior A players were supposed to attend high school, but Goldsworthy and Sanderson were the class clowns. One day they were kept after school as punishment. Refusing to be late for practice, they walked out and never returned.

Goldy was a big awkward player and an ordinary scorer as an amateur. He graduated to the professional ranks in the 1965-66 season and spent his first three seasons bouncing up and down between the majors and minors. He got into only 33 games with the Bruins and scored only six goals. But Wren Blair who had worked for the Bruins remembered Goldsworthy when he was putting together his North Star team.

Bill had two operations on his right knee three months apart his last season in the Boston organization. When the ex-

Bill goes into his famous "Goldie shuffle" after scoring a big goal.

During his feast-and-famine early years, he had an operation on his left knee, nearly lost an eye and was knocked unconscious three times, taking to a helmet after the third time. He also had to overcome a terrible temper and a tendency to fight with any opponent who made him look bad. He sat out 110 penalty minutes his second season and nearly 100 other seasons. He came to curb his outbursts, if he could not completely correct them.

The 6-foot, 200-pound winger was not fancy. He wasn't skillful handling the puck on his stick or passing. He didn't always play the defense he should, although he could check a man murderously when he wanted. But when he got the puck in scoring position, he could shoot wickedly. At his best he was one of the best, and one of the few stars to rise from the grab-bag of has-beens and never-will-bes that started out with expansion teams.

"I remember telling Goldy I'd make a hockey player out of him if it killed both of us," Wren Blair recalled. "For a long time, I wasn't sure I'd make it. I needled him so hard it sometimes came out the other side. He didn't like it. We literally bumped heads sometimes. But some guys you encourage with smiles and kind words and pats on the back and some guys you get going with frowns and taunts and kicks in the backside. Goldy was the second kind, and I grabbed him and dragged out of him what he had in him."

"I always had it," Goldy replied with a grin.

pansion teams drafted from the six established clubs, Goldsworthy was not a prime prospect—he was the 52nd man picked.

Terry Harper

The Los Angeles Kings were playing the Chicago Black Hawks in the Forum in suburban Los Angeles. Stubby Lou Angotti of the Hawks rushed the Kings' goal and the Kings' defenseman, Terry Harper, came across to cut him off. They collided and Angotti went down, head over heels. As one of his legs came up, one skate sliced a deep gash on Harper's cheek.

Harper retired to the sewing circle in the basement of the building, a room with a sort of barber chair, littered with bloody towels, where 15 stitches were sewed into his skin by the house doctor. Then in the rugged tradition of hockey players, he returned to resume his night's work. "We grew up knowing this is the way you do it," he said. "Maybe baseball players grow up knowing you don't play with a jammed thumb."

Now the game was over. The other players had showered and dressed, but

Veteran Terry Harper takes the ice for the up-and-coming Los Angeles Kings.

Terry Harper still sat on the chair in front of his locker, holding an ice bag to his left cheek. He held aside the ice pack for a moment to reveal a nasty-looking wound with dried blood caked onto the stitches.

"I have no idea how many stitches I've had in my career," he said. "I lost track a long time ago. It's in the hundreds by now, I'm sure."

Was he used to it by now?

"Hell, no. It hurts the same now as it did the first time. Some of the guys skip novacaine. Not this guy. I ask for it. If I can get a pain-killer, I take it. It's like a big guy who bangs his head getting into his small car. You've got to get in the car

Harper ties up a man along the boards, waiting for a teammate to get the puck.

and you're gonna whack your head a certain number of times doing it, so you accept it, but you don't like it. You're gonna get cut in this sport, so I accept it, but I don't like it and I've never gotten used to it.

"I've been lucky. My eyes are okay. You worry about your eyes. Some good players are gone from the game because they've lost an eye or the sight in an eye to a stick or a shot. It's not an unusual injury in this sport, though we also get our share of bum knees and bad backs. I'm one of the few who still has all his teeth."

The sweat from his night's exertions had dried on his skin, but the cold moisture from the ice bag ran in little rivers down his jaw and neck as he pressed the bag to his sore cheek.

"The most severe injury I've had was a broken back," he continued. "It happened in my second year in the league. I don't remember who hit me, but I twisted into the boards and dislocated and cracked some little bones in my back. They decided not to operate, and it healed with rest. But for a long time I couldn't sleep very well. I'd have muscle spasms in my back. And I was supposed to wear a metal brace, but I got rid of it as quick as I could. I don't like to play hampered by such things. The back *has* begun to bother me again the last couple of years. I guess I'm getting old."

Harper was born January 27, 1940, in Regina, Saskatchewan, in western Canada. Now, in the 1970s, he was in his 30's. Hockey is a fast, rough game which would seem to call for quick, tough young players. But most players need years of experience before they can be consistently in the right place at the right time, reacting almost instinctively to what has to be done, knowing how to do what's necessary without waste motion.

"If you can survive, you can last a long time," Harper said. He had had two operations on his right knee and recovered. He also severed the tendons on his right hand and lost the full use of his fingers.

"It's not the sort of thing that handicaps me in hockey," he said. "I can grip a stick, which is what I have to do."

The injured hand came when Harper was playing for Montreal. Burly Gilles Marotte of the Kings, who would one day be Harper's teammate, checked Harper heavily into the sideboards, lifting him against the plexiglass atop the boards. The glass is supposed to be shatterproof, but on this night it broke and sliced Harper's hand. Soon after, Terry was sold to Los Angeles and played defense with Marotte. Together they were one of the toughest defensive pairs in the league.

Later, Harper was floored by a sneak punch from Chicago's tough Dan Maloney, one of the toughest fighters in hockey. Before Harper could get revenge, Maloney was traded to the Kings, becoming another tough teammate for Harper and Marotte.

Moving from team to team is part of being an athlete and only a fortunate few escape trades in their careers. Even superstars are often traded after their best playing days have passed.

"Actually, I asked to be traded from Montreal," Harper said. "A player doesn't always get along with his management and if you're unhappy on a team it's wise to go someplace else where you might be happy.

"I played my last few years as an amateur on teams around Montreal and my first ten years as a pro in Montreal, so I'd never had to move before and it was an unsettling experience for me and my family. What could be more different than winter in eastern Canada and winter in southern California? But I asked for it. Oh, I didn't ask to be dealt to Los Angeles. I didn't want to go from a first-place team to a last-place team. But Jack Kent Cooke [the Kings' owner] brought me out and sold me on California. It's a lovely place to live and raise a family. And it's challenging to try to help build a new club into a contender.

"Here, I'm needed. In Montreal they don't need anyone. They have so many good young players always coming along, a guy starts to feel insecure as he gets older.

"But it's quite a change to go from a winner to a loser. In Montreal, we *knew* we were the best. We expected to win every game. If we lost, we figured it was just bad luck. The puck takes crazy bounces and luck decides a lot of these games. In Los Angeles, they knew they weren't the best. They didn't expect to win. When they were ahead they waited for something to happen that would make them lose. They'd been disappointed so much they wouldn't let themselves get their hopes up. They wanted to win, but they had too many doubts and not enough confidence. With a loser, after a while you dread going to the arena. With a winner, you can't wait for the games; you look forward to them like when you were a kid."

The dressing room was almost deserted now. The Kings had lost, and the fans had left in a hurry. Harper stood up, put the ice bag down, and began to strip for his shower. He said, "I don't carry any grudges against Marotte and Maloney. When they become your teammates you forget troubles you've had with them in different uniforms in the past. I played in the Canadiens' uniform a long time, but the minute I put on the Kings' uniform I became part of that team. Your loyalty is to your team and the bosses who pay you."

The 6-foot-1, 200-pounder had been one of the toughest players in the league for years and had some of the fiercest fights. Although slow and awkward, he remained tough and efficient. But with Los Angeles he fought less often.

"When I came up, Canadiens needed a 'cop,' a guy who would 'police' the bad guys on the other teams," he explained. "They were fast and had good shooters, but they were being pushed around. Me and John Ferguson weren't as smooth as the usual Canadiens' players, but they called us up together to toughen the team. We toughened it. I'm a lousy fighter," he laughed, "but I was willing to fight. Ferguson was as tough a player and as good a fighter as anyone's ever been in this league. Between us we did what they wanted us to do. We both became pretty good players, and the Canadiens got back on top.

Chased by Flyer Bobby Clarke, Terry gets ready to clear the puck down the ice.

Harper grapples with a Minnesota North Star for the puck.

"The Kings needed a player. I was glad for the chance to prove I was a player. Now, I'm not much of a fighter. They've got Maloney to take care of their fighting. And the league has changed, too. When you only had five other clubs and played every club 14 times a season, you saw the same guys all the time. If one of them gave you a cheap shot, it was easy to carry the grudge over to the next time you saw him. Now there are 15 other teams and you play them only four or five times a season. So you forget the trouble you had with a guy and cool off before you see him again.

"There used to be only a few rookies breaking in every year and they got tested, not only by the other guys in games, but by their own teammates in practice. It was tough for a little guy or a guy who wasn't so brave to get by. Now so many rookies break in that they don't get tested the same way. They don't have to be as tough to survive.

"And the league changed the rules to penalize the guys who jump into fights, which has cut down on the brawls. It's just as well. It makes for better hockey. I can remember riots that cleared the benches. I can remember brawls that involved every player on both teams and lasted for what seemed like hours with the ice littered with gloves and sticks and garbage thrown by the fans, and the cops having to help the refs restore order. When the game was over no one even remembered the score."

He shook his head, smiling at the memory, and went off to the showers.

Terry Harper was not smooth on the

ice, but he was smooth off it. He was intelligent and articulate about his sport. He made himself an important player without having unusual natural talent. Some seasons he didn't score a goal or make ten assists. But he was an old-fashioned defensive defenseman who know how to use his stick and his body and his head to get between his goal-keeper and the attackers. His job was to keep opposing forwards from the goal, take the puck away from them, and send it to his forwards.

He didn't win many All-Star honors, but he helped his Canadiens win four pennants and five Stanley Cups. In Los Angeles he was helping to build a winning team, and was named its captain. In 1973-74, Harper led his new team to its greatest year. He and another former Canadien, the great goalie Rogatien Vachon, helped the Kings achieve a better defensive record than even the mighty team from Montreal. Los Angeles finished the season in third place, making the Stanley Cup playoffs for the first time.

Bobby Orr revolutionized the role of the defenseman, showing that he could be an offensive threat with his fast skating, fancy passing and sharp shooting. But Terry Harper and others like him showed the continuing value of old-fashioned defensive play.

Returning from his shower, Harper started to get dressed. His face was swollen and it was clear that the cut would leave new scars. But he said, "It's still fun for me, after all these years. It's tough, sure, but it's not so bad. When I'm healthy, I still look forward to the games as much as when I was a kid starting out. Sure there's pressure, but for a pro the fun comes from playing the games. If you can win, it's wonderful. For a while, you're a kid again. You think you'll never really grow old."

Paul Henderson

It was the third game of the eight-game international hockey series between Canada and Russia in September 1972. Paul Henderson, recruited for Team Canada from the Toronto Maple Leafs, swept in on left wing with the puck and drilled a shot past Soviet goalie Vladislav Tretiak to tie the contest at 4-4. Later in the game, the 29-year-old Henderson almost scored the winning goal, but the acrobatic Tretiak somehow got to the puck. The tense, exciting struggle ended in a 4-4 tie.

In the first four games, all played in Canada, the Soviet team had won two, tied one and lost one. Canadians were angry and amazed that the top professionals in the NHL could not defeat the Russians' "amateur" National Team. When the series shifted to Moscow, the Russians won the first of the final four games. They had a 3-1-1 lead with only three games to play. To win the series, the Canadians would have to win every game. More than 3,000 Canadians flew to Moscow to cheer their team on, and millions more would be watching on television. The pressure on the star-studded Team Canada squad was unbelievable.

In the sixth game, however, Henderson darted past a Soviet defender and hammered home a goal midway through a contest that proved to be the winner. Canada won 3-2. "I am thrilled," Henderson said later. "We're still alive."

With seconds to play in the eighth game of the Canada–USSR series, Henderson shoots . . .

In the seventh game, the score was tied with just over two minutes to play. Henderson got the puck, outraced a Russian defenseman, lunged forward, fell, and while sliding past the left of the goal on his stomach reached out with his stick and nudged the puck past the goalie. Team Canada had won again, 4-3, and evened the series. "Nothing could top this," an enthusiastic Henderson said after the game.

This set up a dramatic finale. Going into the third period, the Canadians were behind 5-3. Then Phil Esposito scored. A few minutes later, Yvan Cournoyer scored to tie the game. But then time began to run out. With less than a minute left, Esposito and Henderson rushed deep into the Russian zone. Esposito banged a backhander off goalie Tretiak. Henderson rammed the rebound right back at the goaltender. Again the puck came back to Henderson. This time he rifled it past Tretiak and into the net with only 34 seconds left to play. Team Canada had pulled out the series at the last minute

. . . goalie Vladislav Tretiak dives for the puck but misses . . .

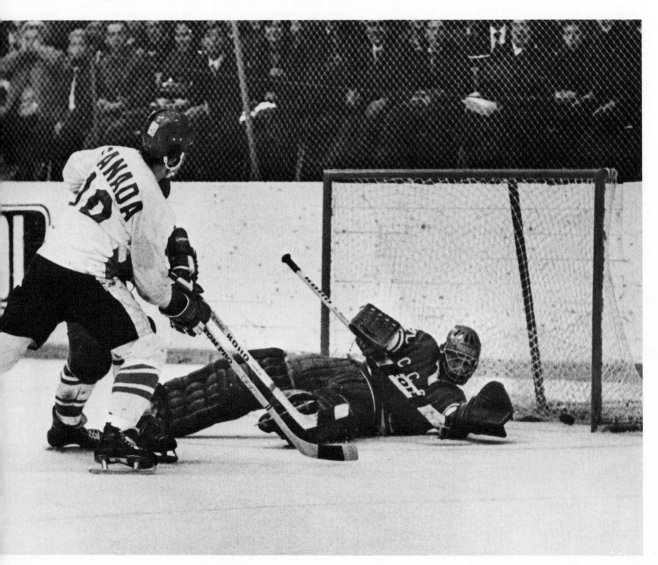

against a formidable Russian team—thanks in large measure to the heroics of Paul Henderson. Wherever Canadians gathered that night, they celebrated that unbelievable 6-5 victory.

"I didn't think anything could top the seventh game, but this one did. I went bonkers," admitted a dazed Henderson, who was surrounded by his teammates in the tumultuous scene in the Canadian dressing room. There had been other heroes, but Henderson was the biggest of all.

Who was Paul Henderson? He was a veteran of ten seasons in the majors, an important scorer for the Toronto Maple Leafs, but not a league-leader or a super-star. He had been a steady player, but less than spectacular. Now in the most avidly followed hockey series ever, Henderson had scored seven goals in the eight games. One of them had tied a game. And when Team Canada needed to win the last three games, he had scored the game-winning goal in all three.

His last-minute heroics pushed Hen-

. . . . and Paul Henderson becomes Canada's hero, winning the game and the series.

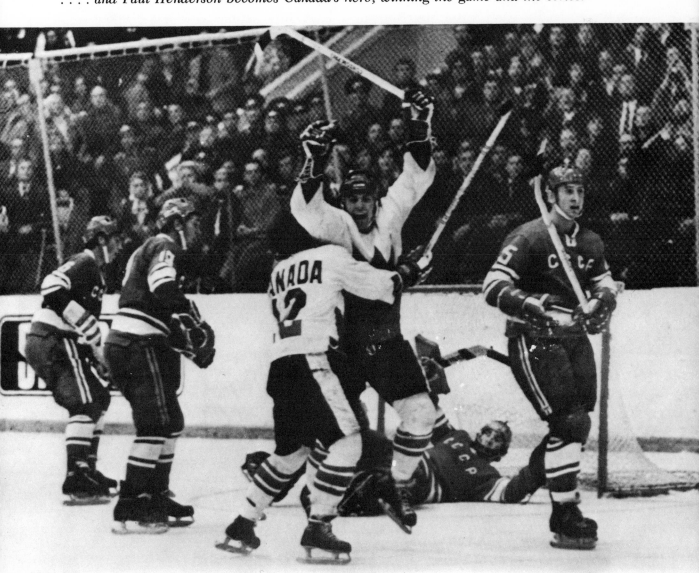

derson into the most searing spotlight any athlete in Canada had ever felt. He was welcomed home with parades. He was given awards. Scores of reporters wanted interviews. His telephone never stopped ringing. The regular season was about to begin and suddenly he felt he was about to break down. Meanwhile, his lawyer was arguing that Henderson deserved a big raise. Paul held out, refusing to report to training camp.

A handsome young man with long curly hair, clear eyes, and a boyish face, he had a wife, three young daughters and a handsome home. He had not been making big money. He only wanted to practice his profession successfully, then retire to lead a good, calm life. But the Canada-Russia series had changed all that.

"Everybody wants to be a hero some time or other in his life," he said, looking back. "As a boy you dream of doing something special. But I suspect if you do it, it never is what you think it will be. I haven't had a moment to myself for a month. I find I don't like all the attention I'm getting. People mean well, but the pressure is dreadful. I had a hot series. It happens sometimes in sports. But I'm no Bobby Hull. I can never be what people think I am right now. I don't know how I can live up to it."

On the advice of the team doctor, he went into seclusion, hiding out with his wife, trying to regain his bearings, disappointing Toronto fans by missing the opening of the season. When he did get back into action, now a $75,000-a-year performer, he could not get back into the groove. The goals came few and far between. For a while, he was slowed by a

A few months after his great deed, a worried Henderson is sidelined with an injury.

pulled groin muscle. But now he was supposed to be some sort of a superman, and fans seemed unwilling to make allowances for injury.

The Maple Leafs had a proud hockey heritage. They had brought the Stanley Cup to Toronto 11 times, four times in the 1960s alone. But in the late 1960s the team began to come apart; by 1972-73, the team was an also-ran. Its followers were furious, and the Leafs, losing more often than they won, were booed. The new hero, Henderson, was booed too. For Henderson, the season that had begun with cheers was collapsing in boos, and it drove him into deep depression. When he tore a shoulder muscle, finishing him for the season, it was like an escape from prison for him. The Leafs failed to make the playoffs.

Henderson sighed and said, "It is like I have been living on a roller coaster. I rose to the most unbelievable high, then sank to the lowest low, all within one season. I was disappointed with my season and with my team's season, but I was so relieved when the season finally ended, you wouldn't believe it. A dream had turned into a nightmare. Maybe someone else could have handled it, but I couldn't. I'm not used to a life like this year."

Paul Garnet Henderson's life was a bit unusual from the beginning, however. On January 28, 1943, he was born on a sled in a blizzard halfway between Kincardine, Ontario, where his mother was living, and Lucknow, where she had been visiting family. His father was overseas fighting in World War II, and his mother was being rushed home to have her baby. She didn't make it. When Paul became a

hero in the Russia-Canada series, both towns laid claim to him.

His father returned when Paul was a boy. But the elder Henderson was a diabetic. He was an invalid at 40 and dead at 48. Paul's mother was left on her own to raise her two sons and a daughter. Paul worked from the age of 14 to help out. The family could barely afford necessities, and Paul had a hockey uniform only because another family was kind enough to give him one.

He loved hockey and was good at it from the beginning. At 15, he scored 78 goals in a 16-game season in one league, scoring 18 goals in one game. The Detroit Red Wings talked him into an early try-out with one of their junior clubs and he signed with them. He scored 49 goals in 48 games with the Hamilton Junior Red Wings in the 1962-63 season and turned pro on a wave of publicity.

After a half-season in the minors, Henderson was moved up to the big club, but he was no great success. Late in his fifth season in Detroit, in March of 1968, he was traded to Toronto. He developed into a top player for the Leafs, scoring 30 and 38 goals the two seasons before being chosen for the Canada-Russia series in 1972. But, after returning from Russia and rejoining the Leafs, he scored only 14 goals in 40 games.

In 1973-74 he scored 24 goals in another injury-plagued campaign as the Leafs started to improve under new coach Red Kelly, qualifying for the 1974 playoffs. Some believed that Henderson, still unhappy, would jump to the WHA to escape the pressure in Toronto.

He had suffered from a series of problems. During the 1966-67 season in

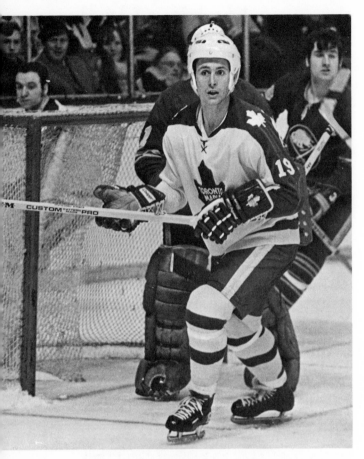

Paul returns to the ice, waiting for the puck in front of the enemy's goal.

the 1972-73 season he was hurt first by a pulled groin muscle, then by another torn shoulder muscle.

At 5-foot-10 and 180 pounds he was not big or brawny. He was not a good stickhandler or a hard shooter. But he was an unusually swift skater and a uniquely accurate shot-maker. Whether his star would ever burn as brightly after Moscow was hard to tell, but first he had to learn to live with his sudden celebrity.

"Suddenly, everyone knew me," he recalled. "Promoters wanted to make my face famous. I was singled out wherever I went. I was pulled this way and that. I'm a family man, but I had little time for my family. My family suffered. I felt for them. I began to feel depressed, tense. I never relaxed. I used to envy the big stars and wonder why they complained sometimes. Now I know why."

Sighing, he concluded, "A couple of weeks changed my whole life. I had those three or four incredible nights, then months of misery. I'll never forget the Russian series, but I wish it could be set aside, at least until my career is over. I can't top it. I could never even come close. I don't think I'd want to. I'd prefer to be just a good player who enjoys a good career and is left alone to enjoy a good life. All I can do is do my best, try to help my team become one of the best again, and hope for the best.

"What I really want," he said plaintively, "is to return to reality."

Detroit, he had an allergic attack in which cold air sent him into a coughing fit. For a man who plays a game on ice, the reaction threatened his career. But it was corrected with medication. The next season, shortly after being traded to Toronto, he tore a muscle in his shoulder. Two seasons later he got a fractured jaw when he was hit by a puck. After that injury he began wearing a helmet. Then in

Bobby Hull

Bobby Hull's jaw was broken. It was wired shut so that he had to drink his meals through a straw. It was hard for him to breathe, much less talk. But he was playing, and blasting in goals. Montreal's mean John Ferguson knocked him down in a game cutting him on his face, then challenged him to fight. Hull jumped up, threw down his stick, tore off his gloves and tore into Ferguson with his fists.

"I knew he had a broken jaw," Ferguson shrugged later. "But if he was fit to play, he was fit to fight. You give no quarter in this game."

When the game was over, Hull walked wearily off the ice, clomping clumsily across a corridor on his high skates. The fans were waiting. He stopped and signed autographs for them and talked to them as best he could. Most other players push through the crowds even when they are

Superstar Bobby Hull was seldom too busy to sign autographs for admiring fans.

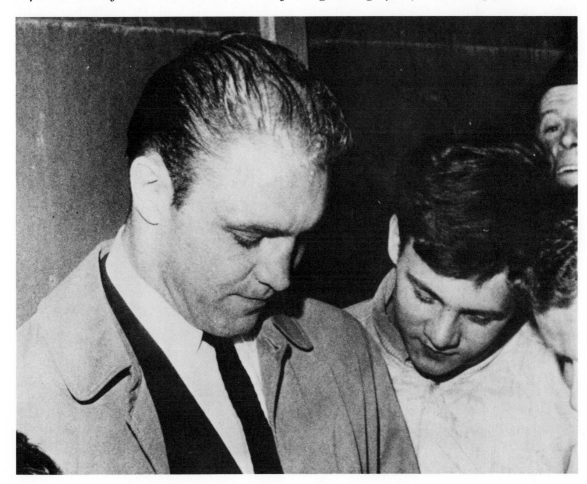

uninjured. But even when it was unreasonable for him to do so, Hull paused for the fans.

Bobby Hull was "The Golden Jet," the most explosive scorer in hockey history, one of its most spectacular performers and greatest gate attractions of all time. For more than 15 years he had been under intense pressure to perform heroics even greater than the ones he had pulled off in the past. He was in demand wherever he went and seldom had a day all to himself.

He must have signed an autograph for every man, woman and child in North America by now. "Twice over," he grinned. He must have heard every question a thousand times. "A hundred thousand times," he said with a smile. His story has been written and re-written hundreds of times, yet he seldom refused an interview. Many nights he sat tired and sweaty in the dressing room, patiently answering questions.

"If I didn't enjoy it, I wouldn't do it. It doesn't bother me," he said. In 1972, after 15 seasons with the Chicago Black Hawks, he signed a multimillion-dollar contract with Winnipeg in the new World Hockey Association. His burden got even heavier. As the first great superstar in the new league, he was called on to play, to coach the Winnipeg team, and to be a leading spokesman for the WHA. Although he was getting older and he tired more easily, he had more responsibility and more contact with fans than ever. "It is something I should do," he maintained. "The sport has brought me everything I have in life. I must put something back into it."

Hull had been a legend almost from the day he broke in as the youngest Black Hawk ever in 1957. He was born Robert Marvin Hull January 3, 1939, in Point St. Anne on the Bay of Quinte in east Ontario. He was the fifth in a family that would someday have eleven children, but the eldest son. His father was a 240-pound mill hand and later a foreman in a cement mill.

Bobby showed awesome skills as a hockey player from the beginning, but it took him a little while to harness them. He was signed by the Chicago organization and played junior hockey at St. Catharines. The Black Hawks were then a last-place team, and Bobby joined them in a hurry. His first two seasons he scored only 13 goals and 18 goals, but in his third season he scored 39. In the next 14 seasons he never scored less than 30.

At his peak he was awesome. He stood 5-foot-10 and weighed 190 pounds. Without his gear he seemed put together with slabs of concrete. He had thickly muscled, powerful arms and legs and a barrel-like chest and neck. He could break a man's hand with his grip. He skated with unmatched strength and speed. As they did with Rocket Richard and other super-scorers, defenders draped themselves all over Hull, pulling him, pushing him, laying on him, often two and three at a time. They taunted him and hurt him with their fists and sticks, trying to distract him, trying to get him to fight instead of skate. Sometimes they could slow him down, but they could never stop him for long.

His scoring rushes were legendary. He would fly down his left wing, swerve suddenly toward the center, draw back his stick and loose the hardest, heaviest shot any goaltender ever handled. He was

After becoming the first man to score 51 goals in a season, Bobby receives an ovation.

accurate with every shot in the book, but it was the famous slapshot that scared people. When it hit defensemen or goal-tenders, it could break bones. When it hit their sticks, the sticks shattered. The Hull slapshot could rip the gloves right off a goalie's hand and carry the glove right into the net. Some said the fear of this shot, which was once clocked at nearly 120 miles per hour, was Bobby's greatest weapon. "Some day he's going to kill someone with his shot," swore goalie Jacques Plante.

Later Hull popularized the curved stick, with a blade hooked so radically that when he shot the puck it did tricks, soaring or dipping or curving, terrifying foes even more. A host of less-skilled imitators took advantage of the new stick, but the NHL finally limited its use, ending the reign of terror for goal-tenders. But the rules change didn't stop Hull. He continued to score 30, 40, even

50 goals a year, playing 30 to 40 minutes a game, almost twice as much as most players. No matter how far ahead, no Black Hawk opponent was ever safe when Bobby Hull played. His broad, handsome face fringed by a full head of blond curls, he was the most dangerous and the most exciting scorer in hockey.

At the age of 23, in his fifth season in the league, Bobby tied the single-season goal-scoring record of 50 set by Rocket Richard in 1945 and matched by "Boom Boom" Geoffrion in 1961. Hull's 50th came on March 25, 1962, in the last game of the season, against the Rangers in New York. Even the enemy fans gave him a standing ovation.

In his ninth season, despite a knee in-jury, Hull set a new record. In January, he scored the 300th goal of his career and on March 12, 1966, he scored his 51st goal of the season. It came against New York in Chicago Stadium, sending 22,000

73

Hawk fans into an unforgettable frenzy that held up the game seven full minutes. Hull went on to score 54 goals. The following season, he tallied 52, despite missing the final few games with an injury. The Hawks finished first in the league for the first time in their history.

In his 11th season, he scored his 400th career goal. In his 12th season, he tied a record by scoring goals in 10 straight games and hit his all-time highs, setting a new record with 58 goals and adding 49 assists for a record-tying 107 points. It was the seventh time he'd led in goals. In his 13th season, he tallied his 500th career goal, following Howe and Richard as the third player to reach that milestone. In his 14th season, he scored his 545th career goal to surpass Richard and soar into second place on the all-time list. In this 15th and final season in Chicago he scored 50 goals for an unprecedented fifth time in his career, scored his 600th career goal, closing at 602.

Hull slams the puck past goalie Gerry Cheevers for his 600th goal in the NHL.

Bobby had won the Hart Trophy as most valuable player in the NHL twice, in 1965 and 1966, and in 1965 he even won the Lady Byng Trophy as the player who best combined sportsmanlike and effective play. He had been ten times first All-Star on left wing and twice second All-Star. He was unanimously conceded the left wing position on hockey's all-time all-star team. Howe and Richard contested for right wing. Howie Morenz, Jean Beliveau and others were close at center. It was difficult to pick two defensemen from Eddie Shore, Doug Harvey, Red Kelly and Bobby Orr. Bill Durnan, Terry Sawchuk and others were regarded equally in goal. But at left wing, Hull was all by himself.

When Hull joined the Hawks they were a last-place team. They had only one last-place season after that and missed the playoffs only twice in his fifteen years. Hull was the base on which a team with such stars as Stan Mikita, defenseman Pierre Pilote, goalies Glenn Hall and Tony Esposito was built. In all his years with the Hawks, Bobby played on only one Stanley Cup winner—in 1961 when he was only 22. The team reached the finals in 1965 and 1971 only to lose by a heartbreakingly small margin.

In the 1968-69 season the Hawks had slipped all the way to sixth place. The next year Bobby was asked by coach Billy Reay to fit himself into a new system stressing defense. Reluctantly, he agreed. But he fit in so well, he helped his side to a first-place finish, its second pennant in his time with them. "It helped me," he admitted sheepishly, later. "Skating my wing more instead of roaming so much, checking my man, disciplined me. I al-ways could play defense. Stressing it made me a complete player. I always could pass and make good plays. I got almost as many scoring opportunities by being in position. It probably prolonged my career. I wasn't all over the ice, wasting energy. I was getting older and had to learn to skate in a straight line instead of in circles."

It was hard for Hull to leave Chicago and the NHL. He was beloved by the capacity crowds of more than 20,000 fans who packed the ancient stadium for every game. Before Bobby arrived, crowds of a few thousand were not uncommon for games in Chicago. Some say he sparked an enthusiasm for the sport throughout the league, helping to make hockey the popular sport it has become.

Although Bobby had had disputes with the Hawk organization and manager Tommy Ivan, he was earning more than $100,000 a season. He and his wife and five children had a handsome house in the Chicago area and a 600-acre farm where he happily retreated in off-seasons. He was no gentleman farmer. He worked from dawn to dusk, pitching hay, milking cows, repairing fences. He was a simple soul at heart and this was the life he loved best. "I play hockey only to pay for the life I want to lead later," he said.

But the World Hockey Association made him an offer in the summer of 1972 he felt he could not refuse. The member teams chipped in to help the Winnipeg Jets offer him a $1,000,000 bonus and a $2,500,000 contract for ten years of service. It was too much money to turn down, too much security for his family and their future.

By leaving, wasn't he hurting the

With a new team and a new league, the Golden Jet sweeps down the ice in 1973.

NHL? "Maybe," he said. "But I'm helping the WHA. And in doing that, I can help hockey. If I can make the league a success, it will open up many more major league playing, managing, coaching and executive positions and increase salaries enormously, spreading our sport across two countries and maybe to more countries in time."

In his first season at Winnipeg he got a late start, missing the first 14 games because of legal complications. Even so, he scored 51 goals, his sixth 50-goal season as a pro, assisted on 52 others and totaled

103 points. As coach and player, he led Winnipeg to the Western Division pennant. In the playoffs, he added nine more goals and 16 more assists and took his Jets to triumphs in the first two rounds before they bowed in the finals.

All the time, he made public appearances, gave speeches, gave interviews, and boosted interest and attendance wherever he went. Gary Davidson, the founder and first president of the rebel league, said later, "He made our league a success. Without him, it would have been difficult to survive. With him, the league seems to have an unlimited future. We needed someone like him, someone of great stature as a symbol for fans and other players to follow. He not only gave us the greatness on the ice we expected, but he gave us more than we expected off the ice. We asked a lot of him and he gave us more. It must have been an incredibly difficult year for him."

Although Hull was a great believer in public relations, he did have words for the men who control hockey. He wondered why the curved stick had been outlawed when the game was looking for more scoring. He criticized the NHL, which favored unlimited expansion for itself, but fought a new league tooth and nail.

And speaking from bitter experience, he complained that neither league was willing to stop overzealous defenders. "The WHA didn't do anything about the way defenses try to stop the big scorers any more than the NHL did," he maintained. "Here are new teams trying to sell tickets by advertising that Bobby Hull is coming to town. And the people who turn out can't even see me with two or three guys hanging all over me. I'm not the first one battered by these tactics. But it's unfair. It takes all the skill from the skilled players. Clean checking is fine, but these octopus tactics are senseless and spoil the sport."

As good as he was, by 1974 Hull was beginning to show his age. He was still there, but he was a man out of his time and place. His thick, curly blond locks had thinned to a few strands atop a balding head. His waist was thickening a bit, and on the ice his body betrayed him sometimes. In his second season with the Jets he was stricken with an ulcer, but the team insisted he keep his coaching job. He still played, driving himself to 52 goals. But the pressure was tremendous, and some thought he would retire or even return to the NHL.

After games, he was exhausted, sitting in the dressing room a long time before finding the strength to undress and shower. But he still sat and talked to reporters. And when he left the darkened dressing room, he still stood and talked to the fans who had waited for him. After one recent game he was tired and it was late, but he was patient, signing autographs and chatting. Somewhere a clock struck midnight, but he was still Bobby Hull.

Dennis Hull

When Bobby Hull left the Chicago Black Hawks before the 1972-73 season to play for Winnipeg in the World Hockey Association, the Hawks were thought to be in sad shape. For 15 years they had depended on the great "Golden Jet."

But Bobby's replacement on the Hawks' top line with Pit Martin and Jim Pappin scored 39 goals and assisted on 51 others. Half in jest, he was called the "Silver Jet," and he was nearly as good as gold.

The old Bobby Hull line with the new replacement was the highest-scoring line in the league with 109 goals, and as a team the Hawks scored more goals in their first season without Bobby than in their last season with him. Best of all, the Hawks were winning. They charged to their third straight Western Division pennant. Then Bobby's replacement really took charge in the playoffs.

The replacement's name was Dennis Hull, Bobby's younger brother. He was in his ninth season with Chicago, but in past years he had taken a back seat to his famous brother. Dennis was a fine player in his own right, as he would show in the 1973 playoffs, but it had always been a special problem to be the kid brother of hockey's greatest.

In the first round of the Stanley Cup series, Dennis had six assists to help the Hawks beat the St. Louis Blues. Then against New York in the semi-finals his pass to Pit Martin fetched the first goal of the series, but the Rangers rallied to win the game. More than 20,000 disappointed Chicagoans returned to their

sprawling stadium for the second game. In the twelfth minute of the first period, Hull hammered a short shot that tore through the mitt of Ranger goalie Ed Giacomin, rolled over his shoulder and into the cage to give the Hawks a 3-0 lead. The Rangers rallied to tie the game. Just when the Black Hawks seemed ready to blow the game, Dennis drove another hard, heavy shot that ripped past substitute goalie Gilles Villemure to put the Hawks ahead to stay.

The teams moved to New York. Dennis set up the first goal as the Hawks won the third game 2-1. A couple of nights later, Hull scored the first goal early, then scored the clincher late in the game with another short, savage shot that beat Giacomin for a 3-1 triumph. The Hawks went back to Chicago leading three games to one. In the fifth game, Dennis Hull scored one goal on a long blast and set up the other three as the Hawks won 4-1, to capture the series.

When the Hawks had clattered clumsily on their high skates to their dressing room, they looked for Dennis Hull, the hero of their upset victory over the Rangers. Now it was Dennis's turn to gain the recognition that had always gone to Bobby. He smiled and said, "It's kinda nice to be your own man."

Bobby Hull had been born in January of 1939. Dennis was born almost six years later, in November of 1944. Within a few years there would be eleven children in the Hull family. Seven were girls and four were boys.

Bobby went off to play Junior A with

Dennis Hull takes the puck from Bob Nevin of the Los Angeles Kings.

the St. Catharines Teepees in the fall of 1955 when Dennis was only eleven. In two seasons there, Bobby became the most promising prospect in his generation. He joined the Black Hawks in the fall of 1957 and by his third season he was one of the biggest stars in the NHL. Dennis was left to follow in his skate-steps.

"There were too many years between us for us to be close as boys," Dennis recalled. "Bobby had already left home and begun his great career when I was just starting out. When I played near home, my dad kept me informed on Bobby's exploits. When I got to St. Catharines, my coach there kept me up to date on him. He did so much every step of the way it was hard to live up to."

Dennis went to St. Catharines in the fall of 1960, just before he turned 16.

Most of the players were four or five years older and they tested the youngster to see if he could measure up to his glamorous brother. He took such a beating that he went home in tears one day and asked his father if he could play under another name somewhere else so he could escape the pressure. But his father insisted he stick it out and try to do honor to the name.

Dennis said, "It was rough because I wasn't ready. The players rode me and a lot of people said I was on the team only because of my name. I started to press. The harder I tried, the worse I played."

He had a strong shot and was a good skater, but the young Dennis Hull lacked coordination and timing. He scored only six goals each of his first two seasons at St. Catharines. In his third season he began to find himself, scoring 19 goals. Then in his fourth season he scored 48 goals, surpassing his brother's best season by 15.

On the strength of this great season, Dennis was sent up to join his big brother on the Black Hawks in the fall of 1964. He was not yet 20 years old, and he arrived with a great reputation. But Bobby had already had his first 50-goal season and there was no way Dennis could cut that kind of figure. The young rookie couldn't get free from major league defenders to unload his big shot. He hit only 10 goals in 55 games his first season.

Worse, his feet always were tangling beneath him, toppling him to the ice. He spent as much time going down and getting up as he did skating. The disappointed fans booed him and ridiculed him.

When Dennis scored only one goal in 25 games the following season, he was sent to St. Louis, which then had a minor league team. He was so depressed he got only 11 goals in 40 games in the Central League.

But Chicago coach Billy Reay was

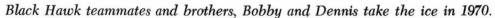

Black Hawk teammates and brothers, Bobby and Dennis take the ice in 1970.

looking after him and brought him back for the 1966-67 season. "I told him when things weren't going too well for him and the fans were giving him a tough time I never would give up on him," Reay later recalled. "I told him when I sent him down to St. Louis that I would bring him back up and he would stick and someday be a star. He did not have Bobby's natural talents, but he had a lot of ability on his own. All he needed was encouragement."

Bobby said, "I felt terrible when things were so tough for Dennis. But what could I do? I couldn't take back the records I'd set, or start playing poorly. All I could do was encourage him. I didn't think it was fair for him to be measured by me. Nobody else was. I told him that. I told him he could be a better player than me in many ways. He was bigger and he was more aware of defense. At that time all I thought of was getting the puck and shooting it, but Dennis played defense as much as offense."

Dennis recalled the days after his return to the Hawks: "I just kept working, and as a year or two or three passed I seemed to mature and gain better control of my movements. At first I felt like putting cotton in my ears so I couldn't hear the fans. They really let me have it. Booing all the time. Then I learned to ignore them. I learned to concentrate completely on what I was doing. And gradually I began to do better."

In '66-67, Dennis scored 25 goals. The next season he fell off to 18. Then he got 30. The season after that he fell back to 17. Finally, in 1970-71, he hit his stride with 40 and added seven goals in the playoffs. That brought him into the spotlight for the first time. "I had become a pretty good player long before that," he said later, "but my scoring had been erratic and the goals are all the fans see. They didn't treat me well and it hardened me. I could care less about them now. I care about the team. I care what the coach and the players think."

Coach Reay said, "Dennis is an honest, hard-working player who can take the tough going. He's durable. He's smart. He plays his position. He plays what we call positional hockey. He makes very few mistakes. He shadows his man. He takes the openings as they present themselves. He has nearly as hard a shot as his brother. If he has a fault, it's a tendency to try too hard. When he starts to slump, he worries and he presses. That's why he has a good year, then a bad year scoring-wise. But he always has a good year playing-wise."

Opposing goaler Gary Edwards said, "He has a good short shot, but he really hurts you with his slapshot. He gets it off fast, on the move, before you can get set for it. It comes in hard and high. It's not as hard as Bobby's, but seems heavier. Maybe because of the sort of shot a player has, the sort of spin he puts on the puck, some shots seem heavier than others. Dennis makes that little rubber disk seem like a heavy hunk of steel. If you get in front of it, it hurts you wherever it hits you."

Dennis still seemed awkward at times, but his shot was still feared by NHL goalies. He was not the sort of marksman who could pick a small opening and thread the puck through it, but he hammered away at the goal. In addition, he began to be a playmaker as well as a

In the 1973 Stanley Cup playoffs Dennis fires the puck at Ranger goalie Ed Giacomin.

scorer. In his early years he didn't earn 20 assists a season. But in 1971-72 he had 39, and the next year 51.

After the 1972-73 season, Dennis's first without his brother, he said, "I miss him. On and off the ice. We had become close. The difference in our ages doesn't matter much now. But it's been good for me. It's put me more on my own. People don't compare me as much to Bobby now. I get more attention now. It builds up my ego. People have been patting me on the back and telling me how great I am. So many have told me they weren't the ones who booed me before that I'm starting to wonder where the ones who booed me went.

"I didn't think Bobby would go to the other league, but he did. I hope he'll come back. But if he doesn't, we've learned we can do the job without him. For a long time we looked to where he used to be. We were used to turning to him to carry us when it counted. But we found out we could carry the load ourselves and it's made us better players and more of a team."

The Hawks were a tough team in the 1973 playoffs. And Dennis, no longer the awkward baby brother, led them. After they eliminated St. Louis and New York, they faced the Montreal Canadiens in the finals.

Dennis got one assist in the first two games, but the Canadiens won both. Montreal coach Scotty Bowman admitted they were defending Dennis especially hard. Claude Larose was assigned to shadow him and said after the second game, "I didn't give him an inch all night. We figured if we stopped him, we stopped them."

Dennis responded to the challenge. He pounded a power-play slapshot past Ken Dryden to open the scoring in the third game, then stole the puck in the closing seconds and put it into an empty Montreal net to cement the first Hawk triumph. He and his teammates were blanked in the fourth game, but in the fifth game, Hull hammered in a tying goal with one of those in-stride slapshots and set up another as the Hawks pulled out a wild 8-7 win.

The sixth game seesawed sensationally. Late in the middle period, Montreal led, 4-3, when Hull slipped a perfect pass to Pit Martin for the tying goal. But in the last period, Montreal's Yvan Cournoyer scored one goal and assisted on another. The Canadiens won the contest 6-4, and took home the Stanley Cup.

Cournoyer surpassed Dennis as the playoffs' leading scorer, 25 points to 24, and was named the most valuable player in the post-season competition.

Dennis could take some consolation in the certainty that he had been the Hawks' most valuable player, both in the season and the playoffs. Entering his tenth season, he had finally shaken off the shadow of his brother. He was doing honor to a great hockey name and now he didn't want to change it.

Dennis takes a shot at Montreal's Ken Dryden in the 1973 playoff finals.

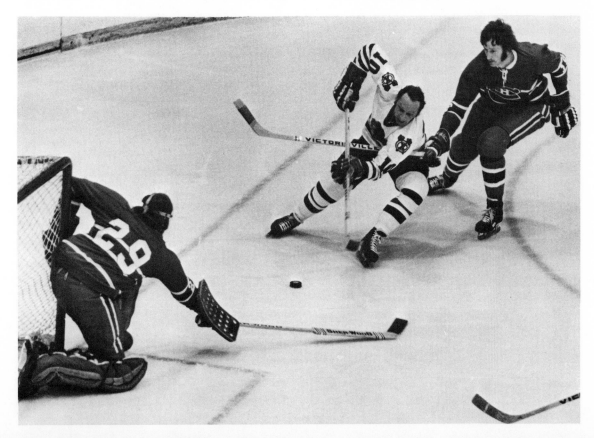

Dave Keon

Toronto's Dave Keon battles New York's Jim Neilson for the puck near the Ranger goal.

David Keon stood 5-foot-9 and weighed only 165 pounds. Even in hockey, where the average player is not a giant, he was small. And like his biblical namesake, Keon had toppled many giants in his distinguished career with the Toronto Maple Leafs. He darted all over the ice, pestering opponents to distraction and doing damage everywhere, playing smart offense, checking bigger men on defense and killing penalties. He was not a super-star, seldom receiving All-Star awards, but he was considered a "player's player," widely admired for his all-round play.

Keon seldom won games with big bursts of scoring, but he could beat a team many ways. His particular skill was killing penalties. Unlike other games, hockey penalizes its players by making them sit out two minutes or more as punishment for breaking the rules. During a penalty one team plays short-handed, five men against six. The team with one "extra" player sets into motion its power play, which is designed to score against the weakened opponent. For a short, spectacular stretch, one team plays almost all offense, the other almost all defense. There are players who seem almost unstoppable on power plays; Phil Esposito scored 28 power-play goals in one season, the league record. And there are players like Dave Keon, who stop the unstoppable players on power plays. Keon held the season record for goals scored when his own team was short-handed with eight.

"The ability to skate, being fast and agile, and the desire to do a job are the most important assets to a penalty-killer," Keon pointed out. "You have to keep after the puck, breaking up plays before they begin, hustling all over the ice, not letting up for a second. You work harder than at any other time. But it's critical because penalties are part of hockey and games are won and lost on power plays and stopping them.

"There's a lot of pressure on you because any mistake you make will likely result in a goal for the other team. Which is why it is dangerous to gamble on a steal of the puck. You have to use your judgment. But you keep control of the puck as much as you can. If you do get it in a position to break away and score, it can be a big goal because it gives your side a lift to get a goal when it is least expecting one, and it breaks the spirit of the other side to give up a goal when they are thinking only of scoring one.

When the Leafs were short-handed, Keon darted here and there, deviling his foes, stealing the puck from them and keeping control of it. He used up valuable seconds by knocking it into the other end when the attackers challenged. And sometimes he broke away, skating to his own end alone with the puck and rifling it past the startled goaltender. He sometimes seemed a phantom, a will-of-the-wisp, darting in and out and among and around bigger, less mobile players.

Red Kelly, who played with Keon and coached him in Toronto, said, "He is not only one of the best penalty-killers I've ever seen, but one of the best all-around players. Despite his lack of size, he plays defense as well as offense. He is very smart and very quick and he takes advantage of every opportunity. He is always around the puck and always doing something with it, making the good play or the good shot. He is as good a skater as there is in the game, and he's tireless. He gives you all he's got all the time. He's just a whale of a hockey player."

Where a Bobby Hull averaged 40 goals a season, Dave Keon averaged 24 goals over 14 years in the majors, with highs of 38 one year and 37 another. But Keon's value couldn't be measured completely in statistics. He was a clever center who set up more goals than he scored and gave up many fewer than he helped to get. Although he was small, he usually led his team in "hits," using his body as well as his head.

"I could change my style of play and become a scorer—that would be no problem," he once said. "But that is not Toronto's type of game, nor is it mine. We play the game expecting to make as few mistakes as possible, aiming to make the other team make mistakes and to be in position to take advantage of them. We play a close-checking game. Forechecking and backchecking is as important as making passes and taking shots.

"Getting goals is sometimes a matter of breaks. Some years the puck goes in for you and some years it doesn't. I've always thought I played some of my finest hockey during the 1967-68 season. I know I've never worked harder. And nothing would go in for me. I got only 11 goals, yet I could look back on it and say I'd had a good year.

"Traditionally, the Leafs have been a careful, defensive team and I believe in that style. There have been free-wheeling clubs like the Canadiens, and you can win that way, too, but when both had talented teams, we won our share from them."

Keon was a key man on Punch Imlach's

Dave cools off after scoring three goals against Montreal in the 1964 playoffs.

Toronto teams which won the Stanley Cup in 1962, 1963 and 1964, then again in 1967. In a crucial game at the end of the 1963 season Keon scored two goals, the last one with eight seconds to go, to tie Montreal, providing the points that captured Toronto's first pennant in 15 years. The biggest single game of his career may have been in the 1964 playoffs when he scored all his team's goals in a 3-1 triumph that knocked the Canadiens out of contention.

Keon twice had seven-goal playoffs. Then in 1967 he scored only three goals, yet was voted the Conn Smythe Trophy as the outstanding performer in the playoffs, a fitting recognition of his all-around value to his team.

David Michael Keon was born March 22, 1940, in the copper-mining community of Noranda, Quebec. Despite his lack of size, he was such a clever player as an amateur that several major league teams wanted rights to him. Detroit wanted to sign him when he was 15 and invited him to join one of their teams, but Dave's mother said he was still too young to leave home. A year later, Toronto invited him to attend prestigious St. Michael's in Toronto, a splendid school with a fine hockey program. He played four full seasons for the famous coach Father David Bauer, studying hard and learning the fundamentals of his sport. Dave jumped right to the majors with the Leafs in the 1960-61 season, and scored 20 goals in 70 games at a time when individual scoring totals were much lower. He won the Calder Memorial Trophy as rookie of the year.

He was a mainstay of the Maple Leafs

Against the Rangers in 1973, Keon reaches past Gene Carr for the puck.

from then on, although he was selected only twice to All-Star teams. He did win the Lady Byng Trophy in both 1962 and 1963, having been charged with only one minor penalty in each of two seasons He averaged only two or three penalties a season—about five minutes in penalty time—throughout his career. He felt that fighting didn't prove anything and that he didn't have to foul to contain his opponents.

"I don't need more size," he said. "What others do with strength, I do with speed. We all must make the most of what we have. People make too much of size in sports. Many little men could suc-

ceed in the different games if they were given a good opportunity, as I was. People also make too much of statistics and of the superstars. I admire the talent of a great player as much as anyone else. But what counts in team sports is team play, and many teams with better players lose to teams of players who play together. I have spent my career trying to fit my talents to my team."

Keon, leader of the Leafs through good years and bad, scored his 297th career goal in 1973 to set a new all-time team record. But it was those four Stanley Cups—reminders of team accomplishment —that he cherished most.

Frank Mahovlich

He sat in the corner of the dressing room, his head bent down, his eyes on the carpet at his feet, his face expressionless. All around him his teammates were moving about, shouting at one another and laughing in the jubilation that follows a victory. But Frank Mahovlich sat still and silent.

He had played a good game this night in 1968. His Detroit Red Wings had beaten the brand-new Los Angeles Kings, and the Los Angeles writers were there to interview the stars of the game. But they were not interviewing him. New to hockey, none of them knew Frank Mahovlich well. They knew he was a top scorer in the NHL and that the late Chicago owner Jim Norris once offered one million dollars for him and was refused. But they also knew that Mahovlich was a moody player who had been hospitalized twice with nervous breakdowns, then traded from Toronto to Detroit. They were afraid to talk to him.

He looked up at them expectantly, then looked away. The writers talked first to one player, then another, and as they passed Mahovlich they hesitated. They seemed embarrassed, not knowing how to approach him. Mahovlich must have known what was happening.

Finally one writer went over and congratulated him on his game. He seemed relieved that someone from the press was speaking to him. A smile spread across his handsome face, but he shrugged off his performance. He mentioned his linemate, the legendary Gordie Howe. "I am

Moody Frank Mahovlich seems lost in thought.

a good player and Howe is a great one," he said. "When Howe plays with a good player he makes him look great."

The writer asked about the pressure on a star player. His answer was that of a man who had always been expected by fans and experts to do a little more than he was able. "Playing well helps everything," he said, choosing his words carefully. "But pressure is not always a matter of how you are playing. You can always play better, you see. At least, *they* think you can, and sometimes you wonder yourself. Sometimes *they* want more from you than you have to give. It seems nothing will ever be enough for *them*.

"You can live with the pressure if you're cut out for it. I suppose I wasn't. I have the body of an athlete and the mind of a librarian. I don't mean smart—I mean maybe I was meant to live a quiet life. I can be alone. I don't like crowds. It is not so bad in Detroit. They are good hockey fans, but the sport is not to them what it is to Canadians. If you play for Toronto, everywhere you go, everyone knows you, and talks to you, and wants something from you, and is a critic. In Detroit, away from the rink, you are left alone."

Then was he happy about being traded from Toronto to Detroit? "Oh, yes," he said. "It is a relief, like being reborn. I started all over again here. It is all new. I am happy."

Francis William Mahovlich was born in the mining town of Timmins, Ontario, January 10, 1938. His father had come to Canada from Croatia, now part of Yugoslavia, in the early 1930s. Theirs was a neighborhood of immigrants, who spoke their original language most of the time. The elder Mahovlich farmed for a while, then became a gold miner. It was a hard, dangerous life. He came home dirty and exhausted night after night.

Frank got his first interest in hockey from an uncle who loved the sport. He began to play on a frozen stretch of swamp across from the little wooden house his father had built with his own hands. His first skates were cast-offs from an older friend, and Frank had to wear four pairs of socks to make them fit.

Frank grew fast and it turned out he had natural talent for hockey. Soon he was playing not only with boys his own age, but with older boys. At one time he was playing for his school's junior and intermediate leagues at the same time. He remembered playing one day in three games—one junior, one intermediate and one senior.

The Detroit Red Wings were so eager to have young Frank that they tried to gain sponsorship of his school team to gain negotiation rights to him. But the five other NHL teams of the time were after him, too. They all sent scouts around to get to know his family. Frank's father enjoyed the attention—he put the scouts off without an answer so that they would keep coming around. Finally a Toronto scout sold him on signing his son with the Maple Leafs on the promise that Frank would study and play hockey for St. Michael's, a highly respected Catholic school in Toronto famous both for its strong academic program and its tough junior hockey team. At St. Mike's Frank led a quiet life off the hockey team, but he gained ever wider notice on the rink. In his last season as an amateur he led the Ontario Hockey Association Junior A circuit with 52 goals in 49 games. Then he moved right up to the Maple Leafs, at the age of 18, praised as the most promising young player since Gordie Howe.

He justified the publicity by scoring 20 goals in his first season, 1956-57, winning rookie of the year honors.

Young Mahovlich had an unusually long reach. He could out-skate or out-muscle defenses, he was too big and strong to be shoved out of a play, he knew how to make a shot or pass in a tangle of traffic and his shot was like a cannonball. Everyone agreed he had amazing raw ability. But even then he was a reserved, moody youngster, very intense but unsure of himself. He seemed nervous and uncomfortable in the spotlight.

His coach, Billy Reay, said, "I don't say he's going to be a good hockey player. I say he's going to be great."

Looking back years later, Frank said, "They wanted me to be Moses. They wanted me to lead them out of the wilderness. And I was only 19 years old."

For a couple of seasons, he didn't seem to improve. Then in the 1960-61 season, he seemed to find himself. His shots began to go in and he began to gain confidence. At mid-season he was well ahead of the pace "Rocket" Richard had set when he had scored his record 50 goals in a single season. The press started to follow "The Big M" wherever he went. He was in constant demand, endlessly interviewed and photographed. Meanwhile, in Montreal, Bernie "Boom Boom" Geoffrion picked up the pace and began to close in on both Mahovlich and the Richard record. There was considerable controversy between the rival Canadian cities as to whose star would make it. The pressure increased.

Geoffrion was an accomplished veteran of 30, Mahovlich a developing star of 23. Mahovlich finished with 48 for the season. Geoffrion reached 50. Geoffrion was hailed as a hero for tying the record. Mahovlich was considered a flop for falling short. He'd had one of the greatest seasons in hockey history, but it was not quite great enough for *them*—the rabid hockey fans of Toronto.

Meanwhile, Frank was having trouble with coaches. He had fallen out with Reay, and now he was quarreling with the new Maple Leaf coach, Punch Imlach. Imlach was a coach who drove his players, needling them and challenging them to show their stuff. He got a lot from his teams, but many players disliked or even hated him.

Imlach needled Mahovlich more than the rest. "Frank doesn't work hard enough," he said. "I've got to give him a kick in the pants to get him going. Hockey is mostly a streetcar named desire. Sometimes Frank doesn't catch it."

After Mahovlich was traded to Detroit, Imlach said, "Kicking didn't work. I tried pats on the back. Nothing worked. He was good, but he could have been great. And that kind of player frustrates a coach."

As a young star at Toronto, Frank makes the ice fly for a photographer.

Playing for the Red Wings in 1970, Frank takes the puck from goalie Gerry Cheevers.

Frank said, sadly, "He just wouldn't leave me alone."

Mahovlich began to slip into shadows. His performance fell off. The next two years he scored around 30 goals a season. The team started to win, taking the Stanley Cup both years, and he contributed, but he was not a leader and he was not the star many expected him to be. The Maple Leaf fans had lots to cheer about in those years, but they didn't cheer everyone. Frank Mahovlich was booed by the hometown crowds, and he began to withdraw further inside himself.

In November of 1964, just after a big game, Mahovlich entered a Toronto hospital. In sports, the physical ailments of players are usually common knowledge. But this time the team and Frank's family refused to comment on the reason for his hospital stay. Reporters soon were speculating that the problem was psychologi-cal, not physical. Some time later it was revealed he had suffered some sort of nervous breakdown.

His teammates were not surprised. Veteran Bobby Baun later said, "All the years I spent with him in Toronto I didn't say 20 words to him and he didn't say 20 words to me. I never could understand him. Nobody on the squad did. So it was easier to just stay away from him off the ice."

Mahovlich returned to action a month later, even more isolated from his teammates. He played well only at times that season, although the Leafs won the Stanley Cup for the third straight time. The next few seasons, he was erratic—sometimes brilliant, sometimes mediocre.

The Leafs barely made the playoffs in 1967, but then they all played brilliantly to win the Cup—all except Mahovlich.

Off to a slow start the following season,

Frank's younger brother Peter, a teammate on the Canadiens, plays a joke for the camera.

no longer talking to his coach, seldom saying much to his teammates, cut off from fans and writers, he sank deeper into depression. Then in December he just walked off a team train and back into a hospital. This time it was admitted he was suffering from "acute tension and depression." No longer shrouded in secrecy, his problems were regarded sympathetically. He returned to action again within a few weeks, but by then it seemed best to get him away from Toronto and give

him a new start. In January 1968 he was traded to Detroit.

With the Red Wings he played on the first line with Gordie Howe and center Alex Delvecchio. He was cheered by his new fans and he seemed to be getting a grip on himself. "Here, at least, we can laugh," he said. "It is not as it was in Toronto. It is not all work and no play. Here, winning is important, but there, losing was like dying."

In 1968-69, Frank scored 49 goals (50

just escaped him again). Howe scored 42, Delvecchio 24. Their 115 goals set a record (which was later broken) for one line in one season.

But the Red Wings were struggling as a team, finishing fifth or sixth every season, and owner Bruce Norris was dissatisfied. Soon coaches were coming and going with regularity. Then the Red Wings began a rebuilding campaign and began trading stars. Frank's play had fallen off, and in January 1971, three years after arriving in Detroit, he was traded to Montreal.

Suddenly he was back in a place where the pressure on a hockey player was unrelenting. Shortly after his arrival, he sat in his new team's dressing room and said, "There was a lot of trouble in Detroit. I guess they thought I was part of their trouble and I was traded. Maybe the move will be good for me, maybe not. I think I will be all right," he said.

He responded with determination to the new challenge. In the 1971 playoffs he got hot, leading all scorers with 14 goals (a record) and 27 points in 20 games. The Canadiens captured the Cup. Now he was a hero, hailed finally as one of the genuine superstars in hockey. He scored 43 goals in 1971-72, came back with 38 the next season and scored 31 the season after that. Perhaps more important, he made many more assists, averaging 50 to 55 assists with Montreal. He scored nine goals and assisted on 14 in 17 games when the Canadiens recaptured the Cup in 1973.

Frank's brother, Peter Mahovlich, more than eight years younger, was also playing for Montreal. (They had also played together in Detroit.) Peter was a giant by hockey standards at 6-foot-5 and 205 pounds. He scored around 30 goals a season for the Canadiens, showing many of Frank's talents, but differing almost totally in temperament. Peter was a happy-go-lucky type who took life in stride. One night he sat in the dressing room juggling three pucks from his first major league hat trick. Looking over at his brother, who was changing nearby, he smiled with open admiration and said, "Frank helps me. He couldn't before. There was too much difference in our ages. He was in the NHL when I was just growing up. Now I'm getting to know him and he inspires me. Maybe he takes the game too seriously, but that's no reason people should consider him odd. No one really knows what's going on in anybody's mind. He's had his troubles, maybe, but he's a great player and a great man."

After 18 seasons, Frank Mahovlich had sneaked up on immortality. He had had good years and bad years, ups and downs. He had been overshadowed at left wing by Bobby Hull, but he had been named First All-Star three times and Second All-Star six times. At the end of the 1972-73 season, it came as a surprise to some that he had scored 502 goals, becoming only the fourth man to pass 500. He had produced in playoffs, too, with 50 goals and 115 points. And his teams had won the Stanley Cup six times.

"I'm sort of surprised, myself, to see it all add up as it has," he said, looking back. "Sometimes it seems it's been a long, long time, and sometimes it seems it started only yesterday. I'm getting older, but it's going good in Montreal. I'm more at ease now than I was. If you stay with it, you win sometimes."

Rick Martin

"Shooting is just plain fun in hockey, just like in basketball. You're carrying the puck, feeling it move from the tip to the heel of the blade, skating in on the defensemen, and you make your move. You deke this way or that. You shift right around the defenseman. Suddenly you're in on the goalie. You see him crouching, trying to outguess you, getting ready for you, gliding out a little, maybe, to cut down on the angle. If he makes the first move, you've usually got him. You see the nets behind him. You look for an opening. Then you shoot. As quick as you can. Any shot you have you think will work.

"You don't really have time to think. It has to come sort of instinctive. I don't just shoot for the net like some guys. I think some guys just shoot for the goalie. I look for a hole, maybe a corner. It can be an art. I try to make it an art.

"You watch the puck all the way. Just before it reaches the guy, you know if it's gonna go in. It all takes a split-second, but sometimes it seems like slow motion and you can see it all very clearly. You keep moving in to rap the rebound right back at him in case he gives you one. If you think you've beaten him and he makes some sort of spectacular save just before the puck gets past him, it's like someone suddenly hit you a blow, draining all the breath out of you. But if it gets past him, if it stretches the cord behind him and the goal-judge flashes on that beautiful red light, it's a terrific feeling. You raise your stick and raise right off the ice a little, like you're flying. That big grin comes across your face and the guys

come at you to congratulate you and you can hear the cheers. That's what this game is all about, scoring goals."

Rick Martin, perhaps the best young shooter in hockey, was speaking. Most big scorers have at least one of these qualities: a wide variety of shots, accuracy, quickness in getting the shot off or strength to blast the puck past the goaltender. Martin had all four.

The manager of Martin's Buffalo Sabres, the fabled Punch Imlach, said, "He has more shots than most—even a backhander." And rival coach Vic Stasiuk added, "He's got a hair-trigger on his stick. It's uncanny how quick he shoots that puck. It just touches his stick and one shot or another is flying at the net."

Rogie Vachon, a rival goalie, testified to Martin's accuracy: "You make any mistake and he takes it. You let him see the slightest opening and he'll thread something through it." And another goalie, Lyle Carter, had experienced Rick's strength: "Martin hit me with a shot and I thought it had gone through my skin and stuck in my ribs. I felt it for a month. He's got a hard, heavy shot that can carry your glove right off your hand."

Richard Lionel Martin was born in Montreal on July 26, 1951. His mother was French, and Rick grew up in French-speaking Quebec. But his father was Scotch and gave him his last name. When he first came to prominence around Montreal, hockey commentators gave his name a French pronunciation: *Ri-SHAR Mar-TAN*. But he considered it pretentious

Buffalo Sabre Rick Martin struggles with a Canadien for control of the puck.

and insisted on being plain Rick Martin. He was proud of his French heritage. He went to French-speaking schools and spoke French and English equally well. But his name was English and he kept it that way.

He started playing hockey at eight. When he was 13 he was playing in the bantam and midget leagues at the same time and was the top scorer in both. "I was shooting, shooting, shooting every day," he said. "But I really wanted to be an engineer. I never thought about play-

ing pro until I was 18. I went to Sir George Williams University in Montreal, but dropped out after my freshman year. The opportunities in pro hockey were too good for me to pass up."

Small at 5-foot-11 and 165 pounds, but quick and elusive, he helped the Montreal Junior Canadiens win the Memorial Cup, symbolic of amateur hockey supremacy, two years in a row. One of his teammates the first year was Gil Perreault, a gifted center who became his buddy and lived with the Martin family. Perreault graduated to pro hockey a year ahead of Rick, going to Buffalo as the first choice in the 1970 amateur draft. The second year, the 17-year-old Martin set an Ontario Hockey Association record by scoring 71 goals in 60 games.

In the 1971 draft, Guy Lafleur, Marcel Dionne, Gene Carr and Josh Guevremont were the first four draft choices. Buffalo had the fifth pick and picked Martin, so he was reunited with his pal Perreault, who had scored 38 goals and been voted rookie of the year in 1970-71. In his first year Martin scored 44 goals, a new NHL record for rookies, and became the team's second straight rookie of the year.

Punch Imlach, who had put together Toronto's Stanley Cup teams in the mid-1960s, was the manager at Buffalo. He had picked Perreault and Martin, and he built his team around them, making it the best expansion team in the NHL. He said, "Perreault is the most skilled all-around forward to break into the league in years. Martin is the finest shooter."

An exceptionally intense player, Martin wept when a goal was taken away on an official's ruling during the Sabres' stretch run in the spring of 1973. It was not even his goal—it was Gil Perreault's. But Martin, who seldom said much to officials, was so frustrated tears streamed down his face as he made his protest.

A teammate said, "Rick's like a hungry animal when he gets the puck. You can see in his eyes a burning desire to score. Even in practice, our goalies hate to be on the ice with him. But he could improve his defense a little."

He became a better balanced player his second season, scoring seven fewer

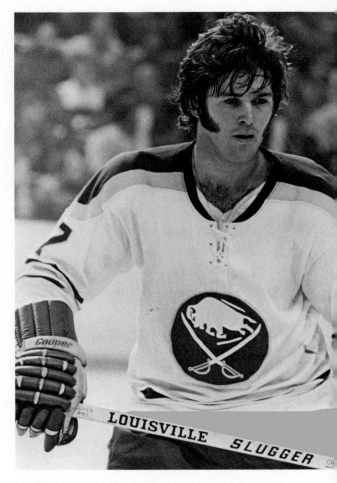

Rick helped make the Sabres one of the most promising new teams in hockey.

goals (37), but six more assists (36). He played on the ferocious "French Connection" Line with Perreault and Rene Robert. Together they scored 103 goals, and were generally regarded as the best young line in the game.

The Sabres surprised everyone by soaring into the 1973 playoffs ahead of established teams. In the first round, they met mighty Montreal. After losing the first two contests, they won the next two, throwing a scare into the Canadiens before bowing in six games. Martin rifled in three goals, including one in each of Buffalo's victories.

Some believed that the brilliant play-making of Gil Perreault was responsible for Rick's success, but rival coach Red Kelly commented, "Each is outstanding on his own. Perreault is marvelous. But Martin is one of the most instinctive natural scorers I've ever seen. He not only is a super-shooter, but a good playmaker and he is getting better defensively. He's a superb skater and exceptionally smart. His eyes seem to dart in every direction. He sees it all in front of him and seems to plan his moves three plays in advance. He helps Perreault as much as Perreault helps him."

Martin proved his talent after Perreault broke a bone in his leg early in the 1973-74 season. Several writers wrote that without Perreault, Martin and the Sabres would hit the skids. The rest of the team felt slighted, and Martin was especially determined to prove otherwise. "It's quite a challenge," he said. Rick assumed the responsibility for leadership of the Sabres. Playing inspired hockey, he scored Buffalo's next six goals over the first three games following the injury to Perreault.

In the fourth game, against the California Golden Seals, with 23 seconds remaining in the first period, Rick drilled a slapshot from 40 feet past goaltender Marv Edwards. Midway in the second period, Rick trailed Tracy Pratt in toward the goal. Pratt pulled the goalie to his left with a fake and fed a pass to Martin, who pounded it into the cords. Midway in the final period, Martin broke up the middle, faked a backhander, flipped the puck onto his forehand side and wristed the winner high up into the net over the goaltender's shoulder. The Sabres won 3-2, and the Buffalo fans stood and cheered Rick for his "hat trick."

In the next game, visiting Montreal had taken a 1-0 lead when Martin burst in on his off-side and banged a short, savage backhander past goalie Wayne Thomas to tie the game. Few players in the game can shoot skillful backhanders, and goalie Thomas was waiting for Martin to shift to his forehand, leaning to that side. When Rick shot backhanded, the goalie was lost. The game ended tied.

The next game, in Vancouver, was a 3-2 loss through no fault of Rick's. In the first period he stole the puck from the Canucks' brilliant Jocelyn Guevremont. Speeding in on goal, he faked goalie Gary Smith so effectively that Gary got his legs crossed and tumbled down as Rick drove the puck over him and into the net. In the second period, on a power play, Martin slapped one from 40 feet away that was simply too hard for Smith to handle. It was his twelfth goal in only six games.

The Sabres did miss Perreault as the season progressed, but no one doubted that Martin had become a star in his own right. Not only was he shooting sensationally, he was making marvelous plays and was much improved on defense. By the time Perreault returned after the 30th game, Martin had 20 goals. By season's end he had 52, joining the exclusive "50" club.

Rick resented publicity which made him appear to be a swinger. "Because I'm a bachelor, am making good money, have a nice car and have a date now and then,

Martin drives in to score against Vancouver goalie Dunc Wilson.

people write I like fast cars and fast women and live fast," he said. "The fact is, I live quietly. I work too hard for what I have to throw it away. You can't help being in the limelight if you're a prominent player, but you can try to avoid being burned by it.

"People don't understand there's no real glamour in sports," Rick continued.

"For the athlete, it becomes a job he does and it's hard work to do it well. He's always under pressure. You can't let up. An athlete has no security. He's on top today, he's nowhere tomorrow. I know I got somewhere sooner than most do, and I want to stay there awhile. But I can't kid myself it'll last forever. I want to be prepared for tomorrow when it comes."

Stan Mikita

The first time Stan Mikita ever saw hockey played, he was an eight-year-old immigrant to Canada watching a boys' pick-up game in the street of St. Catharines, Ontario. When one of the boys handed Stan a hockey stick, he did what came naturally, smacking the boy across the shins with it. "I learned fast," he said later with a laugh.

The great majority of hockey players have always been native-born Canadians. A few have come from the United States, especially in recent years when interest and good age-level competition were growing. But the best prospects still come from cold-weather areas north of the border where the natural ice of outdoor ponds or rinks is plentiful. Those who don't grow up on skates seldom become good enough skaters to make the major leagues.

Stan Mikita was a Czech, but he moved to Canada at a young enough age to grow up with hockey. He was born Stanislas Gvoth on May 20, 1940, near Sokolce, Czechoslovakia, a tiny village near the Tatra Mountains. World War II was raging when Stan was born, and even after it ended, its effects in Czechoslovakia took years to overcome. The country had been overrun first by the Germans, then by the conquering Soviet army. There were shortages of food and housing. Stan's family—his parents, an older brother and himself—lived in two rooms. Outside there was a small shed with a wood stove on which they sometimes cooked, and a barn. There was no indoor plumbing. Nearby

was a small stream in which Stan swam and bathed in the summer and on whose frozen surface he learned to skate in the winters. But soccer was the main sport for the boys of the village.

Stan's family was poor, but he did not know it. Stan's father commuted to a nearby town where he worked in a textile factory. Before he left early in the morning and after he came home late in the afternoon he farmed a small patch of land, raising a little wheat, some potatoes and vegetables.

When Stan was eight, his aunt and uncle, Anna and Joe Mikita, came from their home in Canada for a visit. The Mikitas were childless, and since times were hard in Czechoslovakia, they suggested that maybe Stan would have more opportunity if he were brought up in Canada. The Gvoths took the suggestion seriously, and finally they agreed to let him go. The Mikitas also took a niece from a sister's family back to Canada, and Stan came to consider her his sister.

For an eight-year-old boy, the trip to Canada seemed like a great adventure. But when he had to part from his father and mother and fully realized what was happening, he began to cry and begged to remain. During the long train ride through Czechoslovakia, Germany and France, Stan tried to think of a way to escape and return to Sokolce. But he was afraid to run off, and he sailed from Le Havre, France, for Canada with the Mikitas. He soon began to call them "mom" and "dad." He took their name and they

Dueling with Montreal goalie Ken Dryden in the 1973 playoffs, Mikita tries to score . . .

raised him in St. Catharines, near Toronto, in a house that seemed a palace to him.

He arrived three days before Christmas in 1948. His first day he found his way into that pick-up hockey game. He could not speak a word of English. And the kids on the street sometimes taunted him, calling him "D.P." (the abbreviation for "displaced person," an often uncomplimentary name for the refugees that arrived in North America during and after World War II). Stan understood that he was being insulted, and he often fought with his new "friends." But at the same time, he began to learn English and to excel in sports. He was good at baseball, football, basketball, lacrosse, and especially hockey. He was never very big, but he had exceptional coordination and reflexes and he played intelligently.

Years later he said, "If it weren't for athletic ability, I don't know where I'd be today. I'm not particularly well educated.

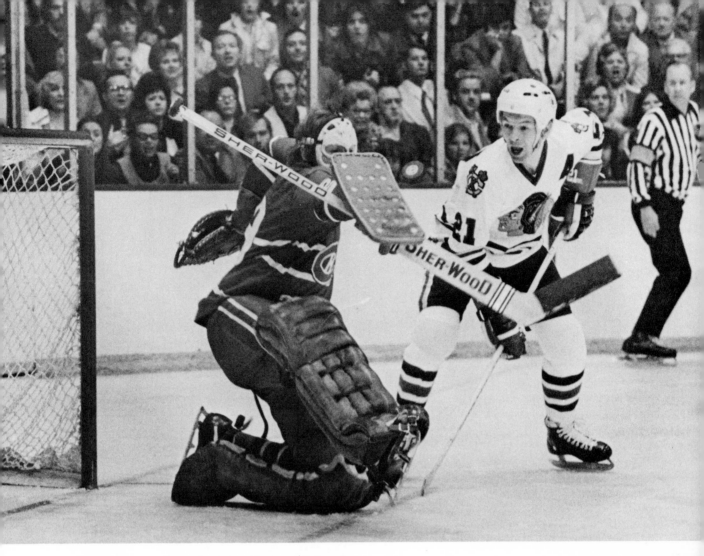

. . . waits for a rebound off Dryden's stick hand . . .

I have no trade. Whatever success I've had has come from an ability to play sports and hockey in particular."

As a teenager Stan was good enough to play for St. Catharines' fine amateur junior team sponsored by the Chicago Black Hawks. In 1958-59 he scored 38 goals and led the Ontario Hockey Association with 59 assists and 97 total points, despite a broken wrist and broken shoulder suffered during the season. He went right from amateur ranks to the majors, breaking in with the Black Hawks in the 1959-60 season. His second season he scored 19 goals as the Hawks finished third. Then he added six goals in twelve playoff games.

In his early years he was famous as a combative player whose temper was on a hair-trigger. Five of his first six seasons in the majors he had close to 100 minutes in penalties. In a semi-final game against Montreal, in the 1961 Stanley Cup play-offs, he got a two-minute penalty for a

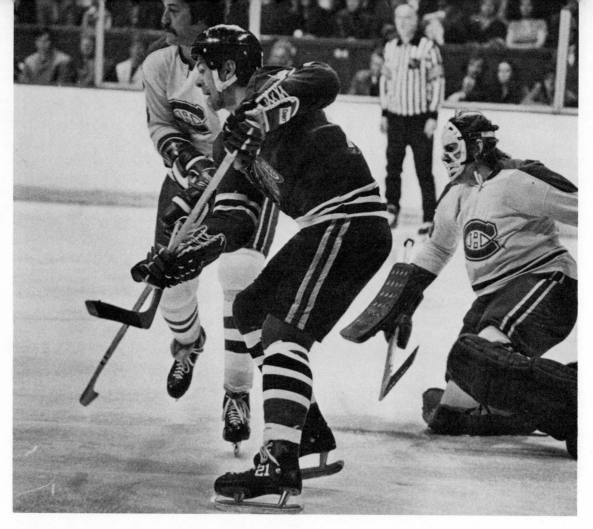

. . . looks for a pass from a Black Hawk teammate . . .

foul, a five-minute major for fighting and a ten-minute misconduct for arguing, all at one time. This set up one of his most memorable accomplishments.

Since there was less time left in the game than he was to serve in the penalty box, Stan went to the dressing room with the Hawks leading 1-0. He took off his uniform and took a shower. But Montreal's Henri Richard tied the game in the last minute to send it into overtime, and when the Hawks got back to the dressing room before the first overtime, coach Rudy Pilous told Stan to get dressed again. He did and got back into action. In the second overtime Mikita was in on a power play and he made a shot which rebounded off the goalie. Chicago's Murray Balfour slammed the puck into the net, and Chicago had won. The Hawks went on to win against Detroit in the finals, taking the Stanley Cup to Chicago for the first time in history. Mikita had scored a record 15 goals in 21 playoff games. In 1963-64 Mikita led the NHL in points. In 1965-66 he led in assists.

Then he came out for the 1966-67 season as a reformed "bad boy." He told reporters that he had come to realize that penalties could only hurt his team. And in the next two seasons he had only 12 and 14 minutes in penalties. More important,

. . . and smiles as the puck finally finds its way into the net.

he had two of the greatest seasons ever seen in the NHL. He was voted the Lady Byng Trophy for sportsmanlike excellence both years, and both years he won the Art Ross Trophy as scoring champion and the Hart Trophy as most valuable player. No player had ever won this triple crown, and Mikita had done it two years in a row.

Only 5-foot-9 and 165 pounds, Stan had become a marvelous skater, a master with the stick, an ingenious playmaker who could put the puck on a teammate's stick in just the right place at just the right time, and an accurate shooter who could score with any kind of shot from

any place through any six-inch gap the goalie would give him. He was perhaps the smartest center of all time and soon became captain of the Black Hawks.

In 1968 Mikita was cross-checked in the small of the back and almost twisted apart. He suffered torn and twisted muscles and other injuries to his spine which were difficult to detect and could not be corrected by surgery. But they began to give him more and more trouble as the years passed and slowed him down considerably.

One night in the 1970s he stood before his dressing-room stall strapping himself into a corset which served as a back brace and spoke about his back. "Since it happened I have not had one day without pain," he said. "It gets so damn sore sometimes I think I can't stand it. It's like a dull toothache. After a night's sleep it stiffens up and I can hardly get out of bed. I struggle up and force myself to move around. I do stretching exercises. I take cortisone shots. And I play. I've been to doctor after doctor but they've been unable to help me. They tell me to take time off regularly to rest it. During the season, how can I? They tell me to wear the corset. But it restricts my movements so sometimes I just take it off and only wear it after games. I can't do everything I could do, but I do the best I can. There is no sentiment in this business. You cut it or they cut you."

After 1969 he had good seasons, but the fans were used to great seasons from him and they even booed him sometimes. He shrugged it off. In 1972, he was picked for Team Canada, which met the Soviet National team, but seldom played. Others who played little packed up and returned home, but Stan would not desert his team and he would not complain. Coach Harry Sinden said, "He could have made me look small, but he's too big a man for that."

When Bobby Hull jumped to the new World Hockey Association before the 1972-73 season, Mikita helped fill the gap, and his Hawks won their fifth regular season title in seven years. He was offered $300,000 a year to jump to the WHA, but in 1973 he signed to remain with the Hawks in the NHL for $200,000 a year. "Maybe it cost me some money," he said, "but this is my league, and it's been good to me."

Stan even tried acupuncture treatments to reduce the pain in his back. He reported that the unorthodox needle treatments worked, and some nights he played like a healthy man again. After 15 seasons he'd averaged 28 goals, 48 assists and 76 points a season. In 1973-74 he broke Bobby Hull's Black Hawk scoring record, finishing the season with 1,154 scoring points. He was assured of a place among the all-time greats of hockey.

Stan and his wife, Jill, had a daughter and a son. After his daughter was born, he used to sneak into her room at night, watch her asleep and wonder how a parent could give a child away. His parents had given him away, and he had gotten the chance to become respected and famous and rich as a hockey player. He had visited the Gvoths in Czechoslovakia several times and insisted that he didn't resent what they did. Still, he wondered if he could do the same thing in the same situation. Thanks to his hockey success, it was a decision he would never have to make.

Jim Neilson

James Anthony Neilson's father was a Danish immigrant, a fur trapper in the wilds of northern Canada. His mother was a full-blooded Cree Indian. Jim was born in Big River, Saskatchewan, on November 28, 1940. As he grew he had the high cheekbones and straight black hair of his Indian ancestors. Years later, when he became a hockey star, it was inevitable that newspapers and his teammates would call him "The Chief."

When Jim was a little boy, his mother left the family and returned to her tribe's reservation. Olaf Neilson was left with a son and two daughters to care for. Their cabin home was far from any town or school, and Jim's father had to spend weeks tending his traps in the wilderness. He decided to place Jim, who was four, and his sisters in St. Patrick's Catholic Orphanage in Prince Albert, Saskatchewan.

Jim's two sisters later left the orphanage and were placed in a private school. But Jim lived at St. Patrick's for the next twelve years.

"We did not have much," he recalled, "but we were fed and clothed well enough. We were kept warm and never went to bed hungry. The nuns were very nice to us. I got very good schooling there and I learned to play hockey."

Neilson grew big and muscular, and he soon became a strong-skating young hockey star. When he left the orphanage,

Veteran Ranger defenseman Jim Neilson carries the puck down the ice.

he played amateur hockey with the Prince Albert Mintos of the Saskatchewan Junior Hockey League, already displaying his talent as a rugged defenseman.

After two years he turned pro in the New York Rangers' organization and broke in with Kitchener-Waterloo of the Eastern Pro League. He was a long way from home, but his playing was spectacular and he was named rookie of the year. In 1962, before his 21st birthday, he reported to the New York Rangers in the National Hockey League. Twelve years later he was still providing them with top defensive hockey.

When he arrived in New York, Neilson was still a clumsy performer, but he was good enough and tough enough to be a regular right from the start. He was paired with aging Doug Harvey, one of hockey's great defensemen who was then near the end of his career. Harvey and another veteran, Harry Howell, took Neilson under their wings and taught him much about big-league hockey. Years later, when Brad Park came up, Neilson had a chance to teach another newcomer. Park said: "A kid makes a lot of mistakes in the majors because he doesn't have all the right moves grooved yet. The major leaguers surprise him by how fast they make their moves, and he's under a lot of pressure trying to prove himself. Every mistake seems to cost him a goal and shakes his confidence. He needs a player like Neilson who's been around, who can point out the proper positions for him to take, who can cover for him, give him advice, encourage him and steady him down. 'The Chief' did it for me."

"What Doug Harvey and Harry Howell passed on to me when I was breaking in, I passed on to Brad Park when he was breaking in," Neilson said. "Brad had so much natural talent he didn't need much, but every new player needs help. Especially the kids who come up today playing like Bobby Orr. A lot of them are natural forwards who play defense like forwards. But a defenseman still has to think defense first and a lot of young defensemen need help on their defensive play or else the great forwards up here will burn them again and again. Unless you have Orr's quickness, you can't get away with what Orr can. You have to play your position properly and always be in the right place at the right time. It takes time to learn this and sometimes a tip or two from a veteran will straighten you out."

Jim was a big 6-foot-2, 200-pounder, and over the years he had learned all the tricks of defensive hockey. He was not a big hitter, but he knew how to maneuver attackers out of a play. He used his stick well, stealing the puck off another player's stick with almost a pickpocket's skill. He could force an opponent into the boards with his stick or his body, take the puck, and skate it out of his zone if a forward was not free to take a pass.

Jim averaged around five goals and 20 assists a season, totals that could not be compared to the totals of Bobby Orr and other modern sharp-shooting defensemen. But until recent years, playing defense was the first job of defensemen, and Neilson was there doing that job even when the sharpshooters fell down, allowing enemy goals that should never have been made. Neilson and other "defensive defensemen" were once the mainstay of a successful hockey team. And even today, when the spotlight has shifted to high-

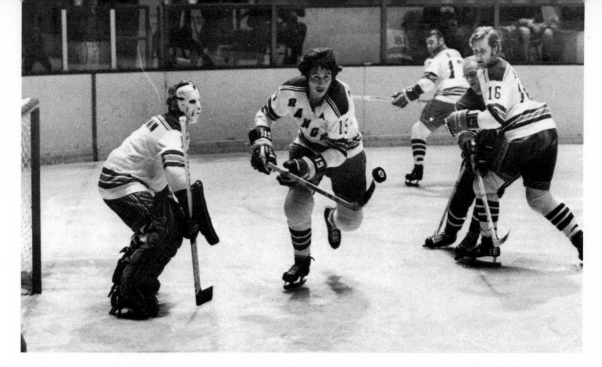

Neilson seems to be balancing the puck on the end of his stick near the Ranger goal.

scoring defensemen, the contribution of sound defensive players—Neilson, Terry, Harper, Bill White and others—is badly underrated. Neilson observed wryly that he got attention when he scored a few goals, but scoring had little to do with whether he had a good season.

In 1966-67, the year Bobby Orr came up to the Boston Bruins, Neilson had such an inconsistent season that he was benched in the playoffs. He was trying to skate with the puck and score goals, but for him it didn't work. He was trying to do things he could not do well. Being benched shook him up, however, and he took a long look at his talents. Once he began to concentrate on playing defense first and offense second, once he began to try to make the good play all the time instead of the game-breaking great play from time to time, he found himself. He bounced back in 1967-68 and made the All-Star team.

He probably hit his peak in the 1971

playoffs. Midway in the first game of the opening round against Toronto, the Rangers were behind 3-1 when Neilson fed Rod Gilbert a pass that produced a goal. The Rangers got rolling, finally winning 5-4. Toronto won the next two games to lead the series, but in the fourth game Neilson fed Bob Nevin for the score that started the Rangers toward a 3-1 triumph that tied the series. Those were the accomplishments that showed in the box scores, but what didn't show was Neilson's determined defensive play. He stood up to enemy rushes, took the puck off the stick of Dave Keon on one breakaway, stole it from Norm Ullman three times deep in New York territory, and hammered Paul Henderson and George Armstrong into the boards to break up other big plays.

In the fifth game in New York, Neilson and Bruce MacGregor collaborated getting the puck to Ted Irvine, who scored to put the Rangers in front and Neilson was tremendous in cracking Toronto rushes throughout the rest of a 3-1 victory. New York won the sixth game 2-1 to wrap up the first round of the playoffs.

Chicago won the semi-finals from New York, but the series went the full seven games. There were times when Neilson seemed to carry the Rangers. In the third game he terrorized the Hawks with a hitting spree from the first that led his club to a critical triumph and put them in front in the series. He deftly lifted the puck from Bobby Hull, who was blazing in on a breakaway. The Madison Square Garden crowd cheered his beautiful play. In the seventh game, he blocked shots by

Bobby and brother Dennis bravely and had a key steal on Cliff Koroll. Chicago scored four goals only twice in seven games and later goalie Ed Giacomin said, "Guys like Jimmy Neilson made it easy for me." Captain Vic Hadfield added, "Jim is a defensive player and playoffs are defensive games. That's why Jim means the most to us when the games mean the most—in the playoffs. He instills a sense of confidence in the rest of the team. It's a bum rap that he doesn't hit enough. He hits when it matters. He doesn't score a ton so he's not a big hero to the fans, but he makes the offensive plays when we need them. What counts is that you know

Neilson and goalie Ed Giacomin sadly watch the puck roll in as two Canadiens cheer.

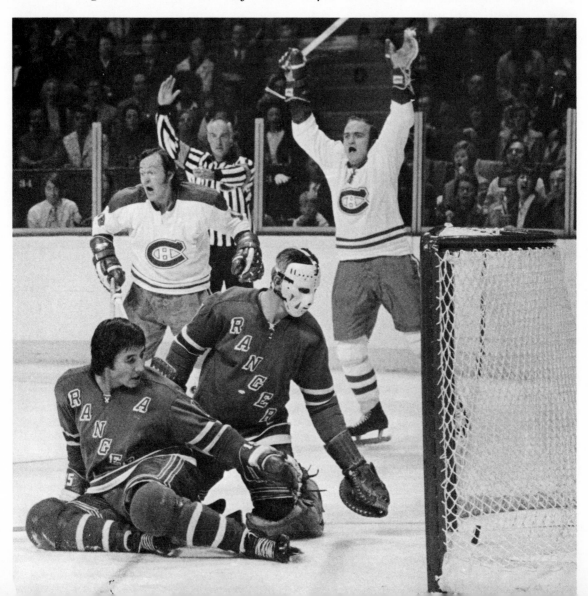

in a tight situation Jimmy's going to control the puck and make the right play with it. He's poised and doesn't panic."

Jim said, "I get tired of hearing I don't hit enough. My temperament is such that I don't fly off the handle and try to take people apart. You make mistakes doing that. When I was younger I'd get overexcited and try for foolish plays and make mistakes. Now I try to play it cool and control myself and my teammates and the game."

In the 1970s Neilson was the senior citizen of the Rangers' strong rear guard and expected to stay at the top among defensive defensemen for some time to come. Despite an injury he was superb in the 1972 playoffs. He got two assists in the fourth game at the Montreal Forum and he stole the puck from Yvan Cournoyer and Jacques Lemaire twice each on breakaways as the Canadiens were removed in a surprising six games. He assisted on New York's only goal in the second game of the finals against Boston and was a model of consistency throughout, although the Bruins won in six games and took the Stanley Cup.

During his career, Neilson had been sidelined by a shoulder separation, stretched knee ligaments, a broken finger and a broken foot. He had elbow surgery and recurring knee problems. Still, he insisted, "I've had no serious injuries. It's a tough game, but I've survived so far and feel fine, like a young man, and love to play."

Neilson and his wife and three children lived in Long Beach, New York, during the season, but still went back to the open spaces of Canada to spend the off-seasons. "I am happy enough in New York," he said. "There is a lot to do and it is exciting. I am somewhat at home there by now. But it is a big city. I still prefer the open spaces, the lakes and fields. I still prefer fresh air and clear skies. I am most at home in the country where I was born and reared. I hunt and fish and teach my children to live with nature."

Jim sometimes visited his father, who had retired. Olaf had never seen his son play big-time hockey, except on television. Jim says, "He lives alone in the wilderness and is content. He was never a hockey fan. He doesn't know much about the game. I know he is proud that I have made it in hockey because it is what I wanted, but I think he is prouder of me as a son than as a hockey player. He knows I make a lot of money now, but money does not mean much to him. I have no hard feelings for him. He was left alone with us and had to scratch out the hardest sort of a living and simply couldn't care for us himself."

Neilson had seen his mother only a few times since he was a small boy. "I have gone to see her sometimes. We just do not have much to say to each other. I'm not sure what she thinks of me, but I do not think hard things about her. She did what she was driven to do. We can't always help ourselves."

He had come a long way from the woods and the orphanage, but he still returned to visit St. Patrick's from time to time. As their most famous graduate he was a hero to those there now. Of course, many youngsters had scratched their way out of small, isolated communities in Canada but it seemed that Jim Neilson had come further than most to succeed at a hard position in a hard game.

Bobby Orr

The winning goal scored, Bobby Orr raises his stick and is tripped from behind.

In the early 1960s the Boston Bruins were a last-place team, and many said Bobby Orr would bring them the Stanley Cup when he grew up. Now in the spring of 1970 he was with them, and they were within one victory of capturing that coveted trophy. But the St. Louis Blues had one of the greatest goaltenders in hockey history, Glenn Hall, and he was frustrat-ing their every offensive move. The teams were tied in sudden-death overtime. The first goal would win it.

The puck was shot into the Blues' zone. As a St. Louis defenseman got the puck and started to clear it out of danger, Orr rushed daringly from his own defense-man's position in the Bruin zone. Reaching out with a little flicking motion of his stick, Orr stole the disk right off the stick of forward Larry Keenan, and back-handed it along the backboards to Derek Sanderson, who had gone behind the Blues' net. Then Orr broke for the front of the net.

Sanderson flipped the puck over a de-fender's stick right back at Bobby, who was skating past the goal from right to left. Orr received the pass and in the in-stant it touched his stick he wristed the puck at a hole Hall had left exposed as he desperately sought to cover up. At the same moment Blues defenseman Noel Picard jammed his stick between Bobby's legs, and as the puck shot past goalie Hall into the net, Orr went flying through the air, his stick held high in his right hand. As the red light flashed on, he crashed to the ice. Before he could get up, his ec-static teammates had poured all over him, hugging him, laughing and some even crying.

The crowd in old Boston Garden roared, for the Stanley Cup was theirs for the first time in 30 years. Bobby had brought it to them. Oh, there were others who had helped, some—like super-scorer Phil Esposito—every bit as much. But it was Bobby who stole the show. He had delivered as advertised, coming through in the clutch. Bobby Orr was the most spectacular player of his generation.

At 22, Bobby was already in his fourth season with the Bruins. He looked younger than his years—his face was boyish and a thick shock of brown hair flapped over his forehead. At 5-foot-11, 185 pounds, he was not a big, brawny young man. But he had strong legs, an uncanny touch, and reflexes and coordination which defied reality. Already some considered him the greatest player who ever lived. He had revolutionized his sport and, in an unpredictable way, done damage to it.

Traditionally, defensemen were heavy, husky, rugged guys. They could not skate as well as forwards, but skating was less important to them. They advanced only as far as the blue line, where they met opposing forwards with murderous bodychecks. When defensemen got the puck, they passed it to one of their forwards. They played defense, the forwards played offense.

A few earlier defensemen had done more. Eddie Shore, the giant Bruin of the 1930s, was as tough as any player in history and as fearless as a man could be. He received nearly 1,000 stitches in his career. He broke his jaw five times and his nose 15 times. He broke his leg, back, hip and collarbone. But he also could skate, handle the puck and shoot it, which separated him from his fellow defensemen. In the 1950s, Doug Harvey came along, a smooth skater who seemed to perform almost effortlessly. He was a superior pointman on the power play and a cornerstone of his teams' defenses. And Red Kelly, who could play forward as well as defense, making plays as well as breaking them up, helped Detroit dominate the league for years.

But it was Bobby Orr who broke the mold, who created an era of offensive defensemen. He could carry the puck on his stick and still skate faster than his foes. He could shift directions in an instant, then with a quick flick of his wrist lay a perfect pass on the stick of a speeding teammate or fire an accurate shot on goal and keep going in to get any rebounds. He was a gambler, roaming far from his assigned position. Yet when his opponents took the puck, Orr was often swift enough to beat them back up ice.

He wasn't the surest of defensemen. Critics complained that he sometimes got trapped out of position. And he wasn't a heavy hitter. But he could play defense with his stick as well as others could play using their sticks and their bodies. He gambled but he was fast and fearless enough to get away with it, even intercepting shots by throwing his body in front of them, risking worse punishment than the goaltenders with their heavy padding.

Maybe he should have been a forward. But he began as a defenseman and stayed there. An attacking defenseman had some advantages over forwards. He was not supposed to stay in one lane as was a winger. The defenseman had the whole ice in front of him when he made his move. And a skater as fast as Bobby could rush the length of the ice, outrunning slower defenders and scoring or setting up a score. Opposing teams soon learned that there was no foolproof defense against such talent.

Bobby soon had a wave of imitators. Every budding defenseman wanted to carry the puck all over the ice and play as much offense as defense. And the game suffered because Bobby's imitators tried to do the same things without the same talent. Many got trapped out of position all the time, leaving their goaltenders defenseless and giving up far more goals than they scored or set up. The traditional defensemen were getting rarer, and while the game was faster, it lost its balance—defense no longer played an equal part. Meanwhile, Bobby Orr went on dominating the game, doing what others could not do. He was unique.

As spectacular as he was on the ice, Orr was absolutely unspectacular off the ice. At first he was shy, being the youngest player in the league. Later he claimed he was no longer shy. But he was still quiet and amazingly unassuming. "I'm not colorful, myself," he said. "I just want to go my way, doing my thing. I'm a private sort of person. I give all of myself in the games. I'm on display every night. That's the only me the people need to know. What I do away from the arena is my business. Too much is made of me, anyway. I'm nothing special as a person."

He made big money, but money seemed to mean little to him. His manager gave him spending money (putting the rest in investments), and he didn't spend it. He dressed well, and dated his share of girls until he was married in 1973, but he lived simply. He seemed comfortable only among his teammates, who liked him for what he was and respected him.

Orr quietly visited orphanages and hospitals, and donated his money to them.

He was angry when his visits attracted publicity, and finally told a reporter, "It's very personal with me. It cuts deep into me and I'd rather not talk about it. Okay, I'm lucky, right? I've been gifted, right? But the world is full of people who've not been gifted, but have had things taken away from them. That knocks me down pretty fast."

Robert Gordon Orr was born March 20, 1948, in Parry Sound, Ontario, a city of 6,000, where the temperature may reach 40 below zero in the winter. He was the third of five children, who lived in an eight-room stucco house. His grandfather was an Irish-born former soccer star and his father was a promising hockey prospect who passed up an opportunity to play top amateur hockey to serve in the Navy during World War II. He returned to raise a family and worked as a packer for an explosives firm. When Bobby was growing up, his mother had to work part-time as a waitress in a coffee shop to help make ends meet, but the family never lacked the necessities.

As a small boy, Bobby took to skates as if he were born in them and began to play in indoor leagues at the local community center at the early age of five. And he moved up fast, always able to play with older and bigger boys. His father recalled, "He had a lot of talent for a little fella and I was proud of him. But he was so small I never thought of him playing pro and I didn't have any idea he was going to get so good. Every time he moved up I thought he'd be embarrassed or maybe get hurt and his mother and me we worried about him, but he always surprised us by how well he did."

Although unspectacular off the ice, Bobby was the most dazzling performer in the game.

At 12, he was starring for a bantam team that qualified for a tournament in Gananoque, 300 miles away. His parents only let him go so far from home reluctantly, but the trip was the turning point in his early career. The Boston Bruins had sent scouts all over Canada in a desperate effort to find talented players who might eventually help the team out of the National Hockey League cellar. Two Bruin men, Lynn Patrick and Wren Blair, were at Gananoque to look at a couple of older,

bigger boys they'd heard about. They had never even heard of Bobby Orr. But as soon as they saw him, they wanted him. He was a sensation. His team lost, but he was voted most valuable player in the tournament.

In those days parents could sign the rights to a youngster away when he was 14. Few were signed that early, but the Bruins wanted Bobby when he was 12. They had to wait, worried that others would find out about him. To stay on the good side of the Orrs, the Bruins invested money in the Parry Sound hockey program, and Wren Blair was assigned to keep in touch with Bobby. Blair went beyond the call of duty, visiting the Orrs so often he became almost a member of the family. Before he was 14, Bobby had been contacted by every team in the league. Local fans considered Toronto their team, and the Maple Leafs considered players in the area their property. But Blair and Boston had gotten there first and they kept the inside track.

In August 1962 Bobby was 14. Blair finally convinced the Orrs to sign Bobby to the Boston negotiation list. His parents felt Bobby was too young to leave home but they reluctantly allowed him to go to join the Oshawa Generals in the amateur leagues on the condition that he live with a good family and be allowed to drive the 300 miles to Parry Sound frequently.

From the first, Bobby was outstanding. By the time he was 15 or 16 many felt he was good enough to play in the NHL, but an agreement between the league and junior hockey prevented him from graduating until he was 18. Meanwhile, tall tales about his ability spread. In his last three years at Oshawa, Bobby averaged 33 goals and 55 assists a season—amazing totals for a defenseman. By the time he turned 18 and joined the Bruins in the fall of 1966, the pressure on him was enormous. Only a superman would be able to do what he was expected to do.

He came close right off. In his rookie season he scored 13 goals and assisted on 28 and he was voted to the second All-Star team. But the Bruins still finished last. However, they were building a big team under the direction of a daring coach, Harry Sinden. Then a big deal brought Phil Esposito, Ken Hodge and Fred Stanfield to Boston for the next season. The Bruins rose to third place, then placed second two years in a row, and finally gained first in 1971.

Orr was tested early. He was singled out and roughed up, but he proved to be a tough fighter, whipping such tough guys as Ted Harris and Reggie Fleming. He suffered a shoulder separation, broken collarbone and torn cartilage in his left knee, which required two operations. He was sidelined almost half his second season and part of his third. However, he went from 11 goals and 21 assists his second season to 21 goals and 64 assists, records for defensemen, his third.

Orr came into his own in 1969-70 at the age of 22. He became the first defenseman ever to win the scoring title. He set new records for defensemen with 33 goals and 87 assists for 120 points. His assists total was a record for players at any position. He was voted most valuable player in the league, then added nine goals and eleven assists in the Stanley Cup playoffs and was voted most valuable player in that series as the Bruins won the Cup.

The following season, he raised his records to 37 goals, 102 assists and 139 points and repeated as MVP. Phil Esposito broke records of his own with 76 goals, 76 assists and 152 points. But the Bruins flopped in the playoffs.

Bobby slipped in the 1972-73 season, but in the playoffs he scored five goals

As Bobby gets the puck, he is surrounded by Canadien defenders.

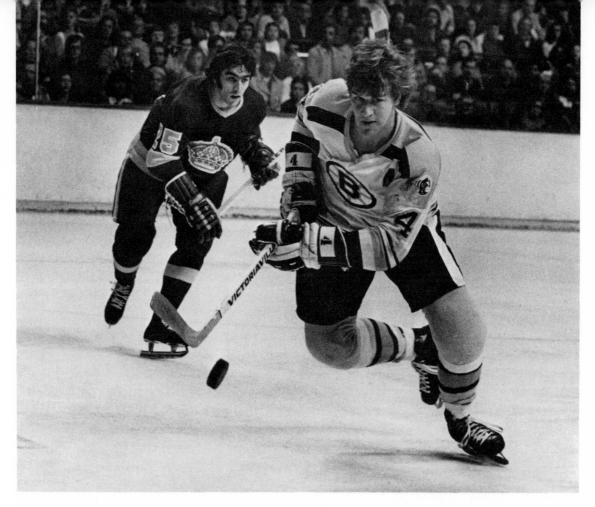

Pursued by Randy Ruta of Los Angeles, Bobby flies down the ice.

and set a record for any position with 19 assists. The Bruins won the Cup for the second time in three years.

By then, his knee was acting up again and required a third operation. Although he seemed to have slowed down a bit, he remained the most spectacular performer in his sport. In 1973-74 he scored 32 goals and set up 90 for 122 points. He was still the only defenseman to score 100 points in a season, and he had done it five years in a row. He had more goals (211), more assists (522), and more total points (733) in eight seasons than any other defenseman had scored in a whole career.

Bobby admitted that his injured knees had slowed him down and caused months of endless pain, but he refused to feel sorry for himself. "Well, others are worse off, for sure. I'm only human, you know. Just a man."

Yet he had almost superhuman gifts of swiftness on skates, instant reactions, coordination and timing. And he had the toughness, both mentally and physically, to overcome awesome obstacles. In hockey, at least, he was off by himself.

Bernie Parent

Little Dave Keon of Toronto skated swiftly down the middle and lifted a hard shot to an open corner at the left of the net. But Bernie Parent, goaltender of the Philadelphia Flyers, thrust his gloved hand up and picked it off. Later, Keon drove again and shot a hard one at the lower right corner. But the goaltender stuck out his stick just in time and swatted it away. Still later Parent batted away a shot and Keon bore in again to take the rebound. Parent was out of position far to his right, leaving the left side uncovered. Keon poked the puck toward the net, and somehow, Parent stuck out his right leg and kicked it aside just before it crossed the scoring line.

Keon was a master with his stick, and a sharpshooter, but his efforts had been spoiled by Parent's sure hands and feet. After his last miss, Dave was so angry that he broke his stick on the ice. Parent stood up and drew a deep breath.

The Maple Leafs kept attacking but Parent and the Flyers kept foiling them. Veteran Norm Ullman wristed a vicious shot from 15 feet and Parent grabbed it with his glove. Paul Henderson sizzled a slapshot from 40 feet and Parent leaped and stopped it with his chest, then grabbed the puck in his glove hand. Protecting a 2-0 lead in the last minute, Parent had to dive out among the swinging sticks and slashing skates in front of the goal to smother a loose puck. Finally the buzzer blew and the Philadelphia fans cheered and applauded as Parent left the ice. The hero was home again.

Parent had won the opening game of the 1973-74 season, returning in a Flyers uniform after two years away. He was overjoyed to be back to the team he had done so well for from 1968 to 1971, but he couldn't be sure the Philly fans would feel the same way. Many considered him irresponsible and disloyal, a greedy gypsy

Bernie Parent (right) compares equipment with his Flyer teammate, Bobby Clarke.

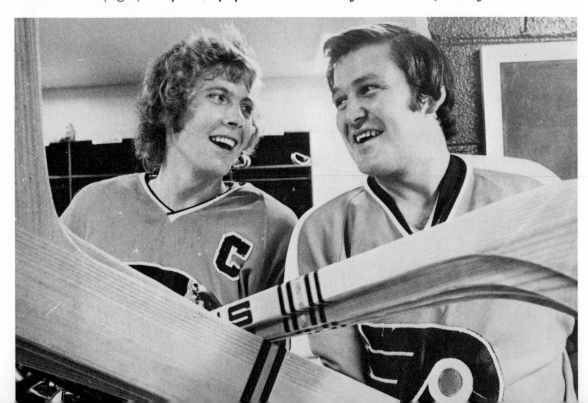

who had wandered the hockey circuit looking out only for himself. Only a few months earlier he had walked out on the Philadelphia Blazers in the middle of the playoffs, and the year before that he had shocked the National Hockey League by becoming the first major figure to jump to the new World Hockey Association. No wonder some of the fans booed him when he appeared on the ice. But winning makes up for a lot in sports, and after that opening shutout, the people cheered.

In the dressing room his teammates surrounded him, pounding his back and shaking his hand. And the 28-year-old veteran with the round, rugged face of a fighter and the squat, stocky build of a football lineman smiled broadly and said, "Hey, it is nice to be home, no?"

Bernard Marcel Parent was born April 3, 1945, in Montreal. His next-door neighbor was the sister of the great goaltender Jacques Plante, whose long career with several NHL teams would make him a legend. Whenever Plante visited his sister, young Bernie hung around, hoping to get a tip or two on playing goal. "Most kids become goalies because they are not good enough skaters to play elsewhere," Parent said. "So it was with me. But I wanted to play goal—in my hometown. I wanted to be like Plante in the nets for the Canadiens."

Somehow, the Canadiens' scouts missed Parent. Instead, he signed with the Boston Bruins and was sent to their Niagara Falls Junior A club. He played two seasons for them, led the Ontario Hockey Association with goals-against averages of 2.86 and 2.58 and, with the help of a rugged defenseman named Gilles Mar-

otte, led them to the Memorial Cup, the top prize in amateur hockey.

The Bruins brought him right up to the top in 1965, but he wasn't ready. He was only 20 and lacked maturity and experience. The Bruins were little help to a young goalie. They were a defenseless last-place outfit whose netminders should have qualified for combat pay.

"Boy, oh boy, the NHL is much harder than junior hockey," Parent said.

If he had been quicker he might have gotten by better. Sometimes a young goalie succeeds on the sheer speed of his reflexes. But Parent wasn't the quickest of kids. His style was to play it smart, and he wasn't smart enough yet.

In his second season, the Bruins sent him to Oklahoma City in the minors. He scored four shutouts and recorded a 2.70 average. Many regarded him as the Bruin backstop of the future. Then in the summer of 1967, the NHL expanded, adding six new teams. All the old teams were permitted to protect only their most prized performers, while the rest would be exposed to a draft by the new clubs. Manager Milt Schmidt of the Bruins shocked some experts by deciding against protecting two of his promising young goaltenders, Parent and Doug Favell. Both were grabbed by the Philadelphia Flyers.

"I was surprised and disappointed, but I realized I'd get a chance to become a regular with a new team and figured maybe it would be for the best," Parent recalled. "After I got there, I found I liked it so much, I never wanted to leave."

Philadelphia liked Bernie, too. All the expansion teams were in their own division that first season, and the Flyers captured the pennant. Bernie was a big reason. He beat out Favell for the first-string job, turned in four shutouts and had a fine 2.49 average. Even when the established teams tested the Flyers, he proved equal to them. The Flyers stressed defense. They didn't score much, but good defensive play and good goaltending got them by.

Parent played most of the games the next two seasons. In 1968-69 the Flyers made the playoffs, but in 1969-70 they collapsed unexpectedly. Two weeks from the finish they were in the running for second place. Then they lost their last six games. Parent didn't give up many goals in these games, but the Flyer offense was scoring even less than its opponents. The last two games were 1-0 heartbreakers, and the only goal was scored in the last game when Parent "lost it in the sun." It was an afternoon game played in Philadelphia's Spectrum, and Bernie was looking into the late afternoon sun which was streaming through the windowed walls late in the game. Minnesota's Barry Gibbs wasn't really shooting. He was just lifting the puck toward the Flyer end from the middle of the rink. It carried 90 feet and sailed by Bernie waist-high.

Parent cried in the dressing room, which was quiet as a morgue. "I just never saw it," he said. With the loss, the Flyers lost out on the playoffs. It was a terrible way to end a season.

After that loss, the Philadelphia management decided defense had to give way to offense. They decided to rebuild with rugged, aggressive attackers. Late the following season, they offered goalie Doug Favell to Toronto as part of a complicated deal which would bring them some strong forwards including Rick MacLeish, who became a 50-goal scorer. But Toronto wanted Bernie Parent instead of Favell.

Reluctantly, the Flyers agreed to let Bernie go. But manager Keith Allen admitted, "I never made a deal I hated to make more. I never had a harder thing to do than telling Parent. I knew he wanted to stay with us. We wanted him with us. But this is business and we felt it was a move we had to make. We weren't going anywhere the way it was."

A press conference was called and tears streamed down Parent's face as he confessed he simply didn't want to go to Toronto. His wife, Carol, came from the Philadelphia area and they had just bought a home in Cherry Hill, New Jersey. Parent said, "I will not be sentimental any more. I will be all business. But my heart remains in Philadelphia."

Toronto's Maple Leafs welcomed him with open arms. He played even better in Toronto than he had in Philadelphia. The team was better, and year by year Bernie was getting better himself. Toronto manager Jim Gregory said, "Parent will be our goalkeeper for years to come."

Then after his first full season in Toronto, Parent's career took another unexpected turn. But this time he made the decision. He became the first big-name NHL player to join the new World Hockey Association, accepting an offer of $150,000 a year from the Miami franchise, more than doubling his previous salary.

But before the team had played a single game, the franchise folded and rights to Parent were assigned to a new Philadelphia franchise—the Blazers. Parent

Unhappy playing in Toronto, Parent still made the saves.

signed with the Blazers for the same money Miami had promised. "It was a matter of money and security for my family's future," Parent said. "But it is wonderful to be back in Philadelphia. I am a Canadian, but all my friends are here."

His start with the Blazers was unlucky and unhappy. Parent broke a bone in his foot in a pre-season game and was sidelined the first six weeks of the season. He was rushed back into action and lost his first five games. By that time, the team seemed hopelessly stuck in last place. However, Parent then began to do better and the team began to win. The team had very little defense, and Parent faced 30 to 40 shots many nights. But he allowed fewer than four goals a game, and in the high-scoring WHA that was good enough. He wound up playing 63 of the 78 games, including the last 58 in a row —an incredible feat of stamina in modern hockey. And he won more games (33)

than any goalie in the league. The Blazers surged up to third place and into the playoffs.

Still, all was not happy. The Blazers played before small crowds in the dingy Civic Center. Parent sometimes went to Flyers games, played before capacity crowds in the shiny new Spectrum. Then, just as the WHA playoffs began, Bernie learned that the money the Blazers had put in a bank to guarantee his next four years' salary had been withdrawn. Even though his team was in a playoff, Bernie walked off the team, earning the hostility of all Blazer fans. The team lost three straight games without him, and was eliminated from competition.

The Blazers were in big financial trouble, and in the off-season they moved to Vancouver. Parent refused to go. The league offered to arrange an even better deal with the nearby New York franchise, but Parent didn't want that either. He went to the Flyers and asked them to take him back. The Flyers finally arranged a deal with Toronto (which still had the NHL rights to Bernie), getting Parent in exchange for his old friend and teammate, Doug Favell.

Parent's career and Favell's had been curiously intertwined. They played together in the Boston Bruin organization at Niagara Falls and Oklahoma City, then were traded together to Philadelphia. Parent played ahead of Favell on the ice, but when he was traded to Toronto, Favell got his chance to excel for the Flyers. Doug admitted he had mixed reactions: "I hated to see a pal go, but I was glad to get to be number one."

Then the Flyers missed the playoffs in the spring of 1972, just as they had in the spring of 1970. This time Favell was the goat, letting a late shot get by him in the last game of the season. The Flyers were looking for Favell's replacement when Bernie Parent came looking for a job. Ironically, Favell went to Toronto just as Parent had two years before.

Favell had been a spectacular goalie to watch and a popular player with the Flyers. He seemed to flop all over making his eye-catching saves. But he lacked Parent's consistency. Bernie had a traditional stand-up stance. "I try to be a machine," he said. "I am not a physical marvel so I learn to play perfect. One of my bosses in the Boston organization, Hap Emms, fined me a dollar a game for every goal

Back with the Flyers, Bernie smothers a shot by Black Hawk John Marks.

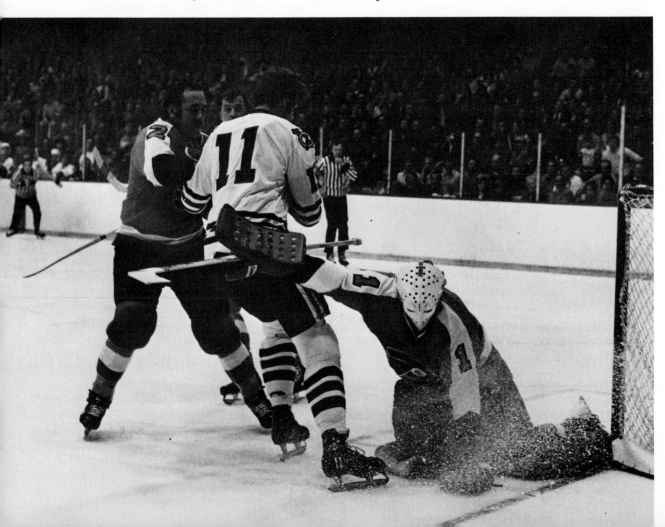

scored when I was down on the ice in the amateurs and then ten dollars a game when I made the majors. That's a lot of money, so I learn to stay up, eh?

"When I was a boy, Jacques Plante gave me tips. When I got to Toronto, he was there—that was one good thing about Toronto. He taught me so much technique he put me three years ahead of myself. So I am ready for every kind of shot.

"I say it doesn't matter what kind of team is in front of me, they pay me to try to stop the puck so I stop the puck. But, before games I begin to get nervous. In the dressing room I shake. Going on the ice, my knees knock. I saw so many shots with the Blazers, I had nightmares. I dream I am stopping pucks and I wake up sweating and can't sleep. It will be better with the Flyers. They have a system in which everyone has to play some defense. I will not see so many shots."

But could he really go home again to the Flyers? The fans and the press were wary of him, and some resented the loss of the more colorful Favell. Bernie answered the question when he scored a shutout in the first regular season game.

The next game he shut out the New York Islanders 6-0. He did not give up a goal until the fourth minute of the third game, the 124th minute of the season. He got another shutout in the eighth game of the season, another in the tenth and another in the twelfth. He was playing game after game and playing exceptionally well. By the 30th game he led the league with seven shutouts and everyone could see he was going to be all right. Flyer coach Fred Shero said, "He has become the greatest goalie in the game today."

He concluded the season leading the league with twelve shutouts and in 73 contests he gave up an average of less than two goals a game. He set a record by tending goal in 47 victories in one season and may have been the biggest reason the Flyers won the pennant.

"I guess I have grown up, both as a player and as a person," Parent reflected. "I admit I made some mistakes in my life. But that is living. And that is growing up. And I will not make the same mistakes again. When I felt I was treated badly, I lost respect for my teams and my sport and I went for myself. The money is important, but I will never let it affect my play. I play game after game, I do not ask for rest, I do not ask for what others get, I just do my best and hope for the best."

In his tenth season in the majors Bernie Parent appeared to be on his best behavior.

Brad Park

Brad Park was on top of the world. At 21 he was the ring leader of the New York Rangers. It was the spring of 1970, and the Rangers seemed to be headed for their first National Hockey League pennant in 28 years. Park was a defenseman, the best new player to break into the big time since Orr. And now, only in his second season, he was one of the outstanding performers in hockey, young or old, and his team was on the march.

"It's a little hard to believe," he said. "Here I am, 21 years old, two years out of the amateurs, playing with and against the best players in hockey—guys I was only reading about just the other day, it seems like—and holding my own. I read how good I am, that I'm one of the best

A star at 21, Brad Park skims along the ice.

players in hockey, and try to keep my head from swelling up like a balloon."

His team was on the road, and he had just finished lunch. He paid the bill and strolled out to the hotel lobby, taking a choice seat to watch the passing parade, especially the girls.

How was life on the road? "It could be worse," he replied. "We could play every night instead of two or three nights a week."

New York treated its sports heroes especially well, tempting them with too much praise, too many dinners, too much night life. How was life at home? Park chuckled. "Pretty good, I've got to admit. I go to places and meet people who were far out of my life not so long ago. But I have to keep it in perspective. I have to keep in shape. There'll be plenty of time to party after the season is over. The season has to come first. I keep waiting for the bubble to burst."

A few days later the Rangers played Detroit and the bubble did burst. Brad collided with Carl Brewer and broke his right ankle. He was out most of the last part of the season and without him the team fell from first to fifth. He returned in time to help them get back into fourth and into the playoffs on the last game of the season. But he was playing below par and New York was eliminated in the first round.

In amateur hockey he had torn cartilage in his left knee and suffered a kidney injury. And later, in the 1970-71 season, the Rangers were in the running for that pennant again, when he reinjured the knee. He missed some games and struggled through others. The Rangers finished second in the standings and lost in the semi-final round of the playoffs. "All I want now is one season when I stay healthy," he sighed.

In 1971-72 he stayed healthy. He was sensational. He scored 24 goals and set up 49 more, which was more than any defenseman except Orr had ever done. Park could skate and handle the stick as few forwards could. He could move the puck out of his end and make the good pass. He had a low, hard southpaw slapshot which was hard to stop.

And he was tough defensively—tougher than Orr, according to many. The 6-foot, 190-pounder played more physically. He had a hip check which could roll a forward right over his back. He led his team in "hits"—checks which carry foes right out of a play. "I enjoy hits more than points," he said. And if infuriated foes wanted to play rough or fight, Brad didn't mind. He took on the biggest and best. "I love to fight," he laughed.

His manager, Emile "Cat" Francis, said, "Park does for us what Orr does for Boston." But Brad was tired of the comparison. "I don't want to be known as the second Bobby Orr," he said. "I want to be the first Brad Park. We both play both ends of the ice, but he plays a little more offense and I play a little more defense. My team scores less goals than Boston does, but we also give up less. Our goalies will win the Vezina Trophy for having the best defensive record. I'm one of the defensemen that has helped them and I'm proud of it. What I'd really be proud of is a pennant and a playoff championship."

The Bruins won the pennant, the Rangers finished second in 1972. The Bruins won the finals of the playoffs from the Rangers. But in those 1972 playoffs, Park proved himself comparable to Orr.

Park came prepared to play. He psyched himself up before games and started out fast, like a sprinter uncoiling from the blocks. He led the quarter-final conquest of Montreal by setting up the first goal in a 3-2 triumph in the first game and the first goal in a 6-4 victory in the fourth game with pinpoint passes. He sparked the semifinal sweep of Chicago, scoring the second goal in the first game and setting up the first goal in the final-game victory.

Which brought the Rangers to Boston. Brad had published a book that season which had some caustic comments about "gutless" Bruins, so they were out to get the cheeky youngster. But Brad held his own. He played 40 minutes of every game. He not only took his regular shifts on the back line, but played on the power play and killed penalties.

New York lost the first two contests in Boston. Then at Madison Square Garden, in the third game, Park picked his opponents to pieces in the first 15 minutes. On power plays he streaked in on the Bruin back line and twice he fired the puck past goalie Gerry Cheevers. Then he accounted for a third goal when he shot a cannonball from 30 feet. Cheevers stopped it, but couldn't hold on. Rod Gilbert rapped the rebound in for an easy score.

When the Bruins tried to get back into the game, Park penetrated their potent power play and stole the puck from Esposito and even Bobby Orr. Then he controlled it with dazzling stick handling

123

and skating, looking like a Harlem Globetrotter on ice, his foes falling all over themselves in an effort to get the rubber from him. Three times Park received standing ovations from the frenzied fans and afterwards, Esposito reluctantly admitted, "Park was the difference" in the 6-2 triumph.

In the next three games, Park played as if inspired. Orr got two goals in one game and one in another, but Brad belted Bobby with brutal checks that stopped him from scoring more. And Esposito was shut out. Every time Phil took his position at the goal mouth, Park pushed and shoved and muscled the muscular forward right out of the play. New York could win only one of the last three and Boston won in six, but Brad had held his own with Bobby.

Before the 1972-73 season, New York signed its stars to huge new contracts to keep them from jumping to the WHA. Park got $200,000 a year, the highest salary on the team and more than Bobby Orr was making. But the Rangers' pennant hopes collapsed early in the season in a game against Philadelphia. Park was ready to shoot and had his weight planted on his right leg when Ed Van Impe dove desperately at him and hit the leg. Brad's leg collapsed and he was carried off. Even though the injury kept him out of action, he insisted on limping through a road trip with the Rangers. He hobbled into a press lounge before one game, sat down, eased his stiff, braced knee out in front of him and laid a hand on it as though to heal it.

"I knew it was gone," he said. "I never even tried to get up. Oh, yeh, it hurt. I was scared right from the first. No one

wants a bad knee. Of course, no one wants a bad anything. But the knees go so far and without the legs, where are you? Not in the National Hockey League.

"It was a relief when the doc said the ligaments were torn some and strained, but could heal with rest and without cutting. I'm supposed to be out six weeks. I suppose I'll worry about it until I can skate and see if I can play on it."

He came back later and it was hard for a while, but the knee got better as the season wore on. He wound up with 10 goals and 43 assists in 52 games. His Rangers finished third. Boston finished second. But by playoff time, Brad was fit, and the Rangers wanted revenge against Boston. The Rangers and Bruins met in the first round of the playoffs. More determined than ever, Brad broke from the gate at top speed again. In the first game he burst by Orr with swift acceleration and a sharp shift in directions and drilled the disk past Jacques Plante in the 16th minute of the first period to tie the contest. Then he slapped another past Plante in the ninth minute of the second period for the winning goal. Later he assisted on another score, and the Rangers won.

His play-making produced New York's first and third goals in the second game. After sweeping the first two games on the road, the Rangers were on their way. Park's pass provided the opening goal in the triumph in the fourth game and the Rangers wrapped it up in the fifth game to eliminate the mighty Bruins. The Rangers themselves were eliminated in the next round, but Brad's play had been brilliant.

Park sighed and said, "Things happen. You dream of getting here, but then you find out just being here isn't enough. When you get hurt and it maybe costs you a championship, it hurts inside, too."

He was born Douglas Bradford Park on June 6, 1948, in Toronto. He seemed destined to play for the Maple Leafs. His dad, an insurance salesman, was also an amateur coach who had Brad on skates at the age of five and in an organized league at the age of seven. Brad played three years for the Toronto Marlboros, a Maple Leaf team in the Junior A leagues, but the Maple Leafs misjudged his potential and let him get away. "I don't know how we could have been so wrong," groaned Leaf official King Clancy less than a year later.

The Rangers drafted Park. He started his first pro season at Buffalo in the Eastern League, but he was so good that after 17 games he was called up. Ranger scout Dennis Ball said, "He is a leader already. The only player who is as cool is Orr."

Brad fights for the puck with Boston Bruin star Phil Esposito.

Pinning Derek Sanderson to the boards, Brad lets Ranger Dave Balon take the puck.

From the beginning of Brad's career, Bobby Orr was the man against whom he was measured. Years later Park said, "He is so good, it is all right. But if he breaks his leg, maybe I am the best."

Meanwhile both Orr and Park were beginning to look over their shoulders at the great young defensemen coming up. Offensive defensemen were in demand, and men like Josh Guevremont of Vancouver and Guy Lapointe of Montreal were playing superbly in the style of Park and Orr. Then in 1973, Denis Potvin, a huge young player with a Fu Manchu mustache, made his debut with the New York Islanders. Experts predicted that Potvin might put all the other defensemen in the shade.

And Brad Park? At 25 he already had lived a lot. He no longer seemed cocky. He sat on a dressing room bench holding an ice bag on an ugly welt on his thigh and he said, "A knee got me. Something always gets me, it seems. Well, I'm still alive and if I can avoid injuries I can do a job. It's hard being a hero sometimes. People expect a lot of me. I have to expect a lot, too. We haven't won anything yet. All I need, all we need, is a little luck."

Gil Perreault

In 1972-73, the Buffalo Sabres were in their second year in the National Hockey League. Playing in a division that included Montreal, Boston, New York, Toronto and Detroit, they didn't seem to have a chance to make the playoffs. But late in the season, they were fighting for fourth place. Coach Punch Imlach was getting the most out of his young team.

Rick Martin was breaking records for NHL rookies, and his "French Connection" Line had scored nearly 100 points. But the real star of the team and the line was center Gilbert Perreault (pronounced *Jeel-BEAR Pear-OH*). In the last two games Perreault scored three goals to help the Sabres clinch a playoff spot.

In the first round the Sabres faced

Buffalo Sabre star Gil Perreault drives down the ice against the Montreal Canadiens.

Montreal's mighty Canadiens, runaway winners of the regular-season pennant. The Canadiens had lost only 10 of 78 games in the regular season and were heavily favored—Buffalo didn't figure to win even one game. It was no surprise when the Canadiens captured the first two games at their famed Forum, despite superb play by Perreault.

In the third game, at Buffalo, Perreault began to apply pressure. He darted in and drove a wrist shot past All-Star goaltender Ken Dryden. A few minutes later he laid a perfect pass on the stick of Rick Martin, and the Sabres had a 2-0 lead. But the Canadiens were relentless attackers, and they broke the game open, winning 5-2. Disappointed, Perreault said as he left Memorial Auditorium, "We are trying. We will just have to try harder."

Winless and within one game of elimination, the Sabres seemed sure to surrender, but Perreault was not a player to give up easily. In game four he provided inspirational leadership which lifted his team above itself. It was written later that he skated "like a man possessed." The score was tied at 1-1 in the 15th minute of the second period when Perreault broke free and ripped a drive past Dryden, putting the Sabres in front. Early in the third period, he got the puck behind the net and flipped a pass in front to Martin, who hammered it home. A little later, Gil unloaded a 60-foot slapshot for another goal. Buffalo won it going away, 5-1, and the home fans cheered loud and long for their hero.

In Montreal for the fifth game, Frank Mahovlich scored early to give the Canadiens the lead. But, just past the midway

Perreault tries to get teammate and friend Rick Martin away from an argument.

point in the contest, Perrault came to life again. Twice he picked the puck off opposing sticks and carried it deep into enemy territory. Then he laid it first on the stick of Martin, then of Rene Robert, on scoring plays, putting the Sabres in front, 2-1. Montreal tied the score in the third period, but Buffalo hung on into sudden-death overtime. In the 10th extra minute, Perreault rushed the net, drawing the defense to him. Then he fired a beautiful pass to Robert, who drove and scored the winning goal.

Back in Buffalo for the sixth game, Canadiens surrounded Perreault with so many foes he seldom could get free. They double-teamed and triple-teamed the talented youngster as a way of wrecking the Sabres' offense. And it worked. Montreal won 4-2 and eliminated the gallant Sabres.

The fans cheered their losers off, impressed by their good showing against a much more powerful and experienced foe, and afterwards Perreault said, "I'm very proud of this team. We gave everything we could."

Montreal coach Scotty Bowman said, "Maybe some thought it would be an easy series, but with Perreault to contain I never said it. He evens things out a lot and made the Canadiens come up with their best stuff." It was quite a tribute to a French-Canadian youngster whose ambition had always been to play for the Canadiens.

He was born Gilbert Perreault in Victoriaville, Quebec, a town in the St. Lawrence Valley, on November 13, 1950. His father was a warehouseman for the Canadian national railroad and a former amateur player. Gil had three brothers, none of whom went on with hockey after they left school. But Gil seemed destined to be a hockey player. He recalled, "I was a rink rat. I hung around hockey all the time, helped scrape the ice, played wherever there was a chance. Jean Beliveau was my ideal. He came from my town. His Montreal Canadiens were my team."

Perreault signed with the Canadiens and played in the amateur leagues with the Montreal Junior Canadiens. He lived with the family of Rick Martin, later his teammate on the "French Connection" Line. His last season as a junior, 1969-70, he scored 51 goals and set up 70 more in 54 games, was voted the most valuable player in the league and was clearly the most promising prospect of the year. He had good size at 5-foot-11 and 195 pounds, he was a swift, smooth skater and a graceful player who could pass and shoot with superlative skill.

If he had come up earlier, he would have been the latest in a long line of French Canadians who became stars for the glamorous Canadiens. Montreal had always had special rights to the French-speaking prospects from Quebec. But in 1970 the team gave up its special rights, so Gil would be the property of the first team that drafted him. The first two to choose were the new expansion teams, Buffalo and Vancouver. They flipped a coin for first pick. Buffalo won, then claimed Perreault. Vancouver general manager Bud Poile admitted, "He was the one we wanted as the star who would make us look better than we were from the start." And Montreal must have regretted losing its claim. Former star "Boom Boom" Geoffrion observed, "This is the sort of player a team can build a winner around."

Gil admitted he had been heartbroken to go with the Sabres instead of the Canadiens, but concluded it might have been for the best. As he said in heavily accented English, "It is like you have a dream all your life as a boy. When you find out it won't come true you are disappointed. But I am no longer the boy. I am grown up. And in Buffalo I get a chance to be in the majors right away and to play regular, which maybe I do not get in Montreal. So maybe it is wise the way it works out and I develop faster this way."

He was a star from the first. Near the end of the season he was approaching the NHL record for goals scored by a rookie. He showed unusual poise as he attracted more and more attention. "There is a lot of pressure," he observed. "But all you can do is your best, no? All that matters is if the team wins. We have not been winning so what I do hasn't satisfied me so far."

Playing despite a back injury, Perreault scored two goals in a game against Vancouver to tie the NHL rookie record of 34 goals. The last was a sizzling slapshot that whistled by the Canucks' goalie. Then a few nights later against the St. Louis Blues, Perreault belted in a backhander from five feet out to set the new standard with his 35th goal. His teammates rushed from the bench to congratulate him, and the 10,000 Buffalo fans rocked the ancient arena with their cheers. All he could say later was, "This is a big thrill for me."

His second season, he scored only 26 goals, but had 48 assists for a total of 74 points. Although his teammate Rick Martin surpassed his record for rookie goals and Chicago's Marcel Dionne bettered his record for rookie points, Perreault was still the big new star of the game.

Gil's manager, Punch Imlach, compared him to other hockey greats: "He's as unselfish as Orr and as much a team player as Beliveau. And he has their sort of rare natural talent. He can skate as well as anyone ever could and can carry the puck on his stick as good as any. I've been around a lot of years and I've never seen a player with his speed and variety of shifts. If he has a fault, it's that he doesn't shoot enough." Buffalo coach Joe Crozier added, "He's already the finest center in hockey and he may become the best player."

Gil was chosen for Team Canada, which played the Soviets in 1972. But he played very little and left the team before the series was over to join the Sabres at training camp. He was criticized for leaving,

Gil waits for a pass in front of North Star goalie Gump Worsley.

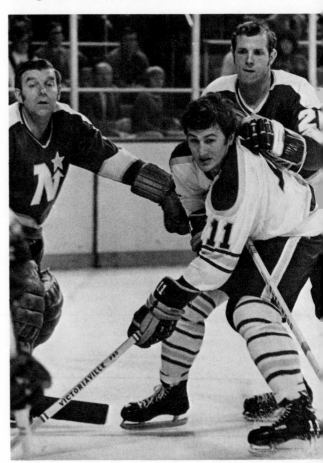

but shrugged and said, "My team needs me more."

In 1972-73 he scored 28 goals, set up 60 and centered the "French Connection" Line, with Martin and Robert on the flanks. Gil took only 234 shots compared to 411 by super-scoring center Phil Esposito, so it wasn't surprising he scored so few of the line's 104 goals. But the Sabres made the playoffs and gained their two playoff victories against the Canadiens.

Perreault was awarded the Lady Byng Trophy as the performer who best combined exceptional play with gentlemanly conduct. He had been penalized only five times and spent only ten minutes in the penalty box during the regular season. But he wasn't afraid to defend himself. When the league's toughest fighter, Dan Maloney, belted him from behind, Gil whirled around and lashed out with a right that broke Maloney's nose.

Early in the 1973-74 season Perrault suffered a broken bone in his leg. But he recovered and returned to action by December. Still, it was not a good season. Gil played in more than 50 games and had 18 goals and 33 assists. But much of the season he played in pain and admitted, "I will be better next year when my legs are better."

He was an extremely reserved and dignified young man who shied from attention. Teammate Martin, Perreault's roommate in Buffalo during 1972-73, said, "He simply is not a swinger. He doesn't have much to say, not about hockey, or anything else. It is impossible to be jealous of him because he doesn't seek the spotlight and would rather pass to me than shoot for himself."

In the summer of 1973 Gil married his hometown sweetheart, Carmen Caron. In his early days in the league, fans used to think that his difficulties with English made him shy and retiring. But even when he had mastered the language and become an established star, he was still a very private person. "Sometimes you would like not to be known," he explained. "People all the time talking about hockey, you get tired of it. I don't want to hear how I am a hero. I love to play. I'm just a player."

Mickey Redmond

As boys, Mickey Redmond and his brother Dick would lay a cardboard box on its side in their cellar, put a bottle behind it and try to shoot a hockey puck into the box hard enough to break the bottle.

"It was difficult to do," Mickey recalled. "You had to really rap it just right. But we'd do it. I'd do it more than Dick. But then, I'm a forward and he's a defenseman," he said with a laugh.

Michael Edward Redmond was born in Kirkland Lake, Ontario, on December 27, 1947, and his brother Richard was born about two years later. Their dad, Eddie, was a former minor league defenseman, who had played with Jean Beliveau on the Quebec Aces and under Wren Blair on the Whitby Dunlops.

"A lot of good kids came out of the Kirkland Lake area to become major leaguers," Mickey said. "Ralph Backstrom, Dick Duff, the three Plager brothers, the two Hillman brothers, and of course, the two Redmond brothers. There were long winters and a lot of ice around there. I learned to skate at three. Later we moved to Peterborough and I started in junior hockey on rinks. Dick was two years behind me, but close enough to be competitive. It helped both of us because we always had someone to practice with.

"Dad gave us a lot of tips, but he left a lot up to us, too. When it was time for me to sign with a professional organization, dad's old pal Wren Blair was scouting for the Boston Bruins and he wanted me to go with them. But I wanted to go with the Montreal Canadiens, so dad signed me with them.

"He built us a couple of big wooden nets when we graduated from cardboard boxes. We put one in the basement and the other one out in the yard, and we practiced all the time. I never stopped practicing my shot, winter or summer. If I didn't have ice and a puck, I shot a rubber ball cut in half. I could shoot before I could play."

After he began playing for the Peterborough junior team, he practiced shooting a heavy metal puck against the walls in the corridors of the practice quarters. It made a fearful racket, but built up his arms and wrists and hands.

"Using that heavy metal puck made a regular puck feel like a quarter," Mickey recalled. Gordie Howe, who was with the Detroit team when Redmond arrived, said Mickey had developed the greatest arm strength he'd ever seen in a young player. And Mickey never stopped improving. Later he built his strength with weight-lifting exercises.

His last two seasons at Peterborough, he scored 92 goals and set up 95 more. He was not as aggressive as he might have been, but when he was skating in on net with the puck, he was almost unstoppable. He was both most valuable player and most gentlemanly player in the Ontario Hockey Association in 1966-67.

The next season he turned pro, playing with the Houston Apollos in the Cen-

Red Wing Mickey Redmond tries to sneak the puck around the corner and into the net.

tral League. He got off to a sizzling start, scoring nine goals in 15 games, and the Canadiens called him up. The rest of that season and all the following season he spent most of his time on the bench.

Then in the semi-finals of the 1969 Stanley Cup playoffs he went into a game against Boston in overtime. He drove on the net, got the puck at the goal-mouth and shot it home to win the game. His stick flung up in the air, a broad smile on his face, he literally danced off the ice to the tune of fans' cheers and teammates' congratulations.

"It was my biggest moment," he said later.

In 1969-70 he got a chance to play regularly, and he made the most of it, scoring 27 goals and 27 assists. However, the Canadiens missed the playoffs for one of the few times in their history and began a crash rebuilding program. Mickey was slowed by an injury the following season and in the spring of 1971 he was traded to Detroit in a deal for Frank Mahovlich. Altogether he scored only 20 goals that season.

The trade was a controversial one. Mahovlich was a proven performer and Redmond was not. But Mickey was young and promising, and many felt Montreal had made a mistake. Mickey said, "The trade was a shock because the Canadiens told me I was in their plans for years to come. It was a disappointment because I always wanted to play for them. But it has worked out. Detroit gave me the playing time I needed to develop. They needed me, while the Canadiens did not. Being needed brings out the best in you."

He started the 1971-72 season slowly, but came on with a rush at mid-season. Late in December he blasted two goals in a victory over Buffalo. On New Year's Eve, he shot in two more in a win against California. In the first game of the New Year, he ripped in another pair in an upset of visiting Montreal. The next game he rifled in two more. His team had been slumping, but they won four in a row, thanks to his eight goals. The Wings got going when Mickey got going. They came from far back, but narrowly missed a playoff slot. Mickey wound up with 42 goals.

The following season he started slowly again, then ran off a string of 18 goals in 11 games. His former coach, Johnny Wilson, said, "He's dedicated, but he gets disgusted quickly when things go wrong and tends to get down on himself too

quickly. But when he gets some breaks and gets going good, he's almost impossible to stop."

Mickey admitted that he was a streaky player. He seeemed to start slowly almost every season, then scored his goals in bursts. "Confidence is half the battle," he said. "I get impatient sometimes and try to drive the puck right through the goalie. When I take my time and pick my spots, I do better. But it's a game of breaks, of ups and downs.

"The first part of the '72-73 season, everything I shot seemed to catch the tip of the goalie's skate or stick or the corner of his pad or one of the goalposts or the cross-bar. I was determined to keep shooting. I figured sooner or later they'd start going in."

They did. Suddenly, the puck seemed to have eyes. It found its way through any available opening. Off on his spree, Redmond mounted a drive the last part of the season that brought him near the magic 50 mark.

Driving toward that milestone, he was deprived of one goal in Philadelphia when the referee said he'd kicked the puck into the net and lost two more when referees said they hadn't crossed the goal-line. Films later showed Mickey deserved all three. But he didn't complain, saying the lost goals were "bad luck in a game of luck."

Late in the season, in a game at Toronto's Maple Leaf Gardens, he planted himself at the goal-mouth as Gary Bergman fired a slapshot. As the puck sizzled toward him, Mickey stuck out his stick and deflected it neatly past goalie Ron Low for his 50th goal of the season. Deflecting shots was an art in itself, and

Playing for the Canadiens, Redmond congratulates Pete Mahovlich on a goal.

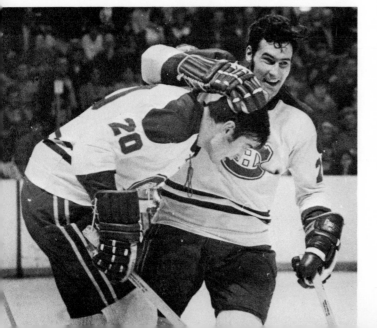

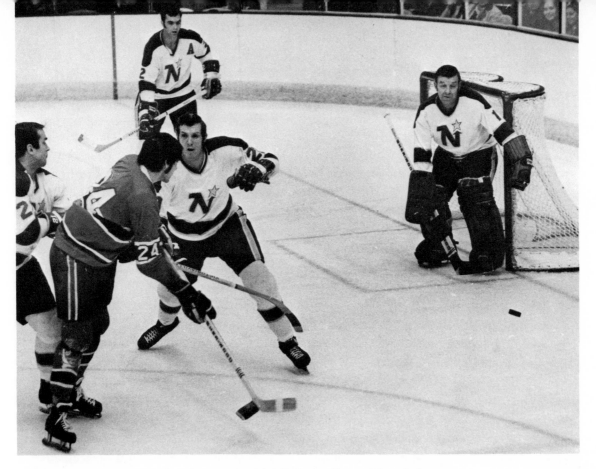

Mickey's shot against the Minnesota North Stars flies wide of the net.

Mickey had learned to follow the flight of the shot, angle his stick just right and bank the puck into the net. Such a deflection was almost impossible for a goalie to stop.

Eighteen seconds later, Redmond drove goalward, collected a lead pass from Jim McKenney and, with a flick of his wrists, rapped a low shot past the goalie for number 51. Although the score was against their team, many of the Toronto fans stood to cheer Redmond's accomplishment, and his teammates spilled off the bench to congratulate him. Mickey seemed the least excited person in the place, but later he conceded the goal gave him "a great sense of achievement."

He stood outside the dressing room door later, dressed in flared pants and a brightly colored checked sports coat. "I suppose something like this establishes you," he said. "I just wish the team was winning. It takes something from it. The team being down drags me down."

Mickey added another goal before the schedule concluded to give him 52 for the season. He also wound up with 41 assists. After the season, he refused an offer from the WHA of $200,000 a year. He signed a long-term contract with Detroit for nearly as much, saying he felt more secure in the NHL and wanted to stay with the best.

In the 1973-74 season, Redmond proved himself one of the game's superstars, topping the 50-goal mark for the second straight year with 51. Along with such other young hot-shots as Rick Martin, and the WHA's Danny Lawson and

Mike Walton, Redmond was leading the way to a new, higher-scoring brand of hockey.

There was no telling how high Redmond or the others would go. But Gordie Howe, an authority on scoring, said, "Redmond probably has as high a scoring potential as any young player in hockey. He shoots as hard as Bobby Hull and gets his shot off in a hurry. He's not big, but he's tremendously strong. His big season was no surprise to me."

Was it a surprise to Redmond, himself? "It was more than I expected, sooner than I expected, but I always knew I could score goals." He smiled and said, "All that practice against cardboard boxes and wooden goals and cement corridors paid off."

The 5-foot-11, 185-pound Redmond was a strong skater, but not a clever puck-carrier. His strength was in his arms, not his body, and he couldn't barge over people. He had to be set up. But if a team got the puck to him, he had a low wrist shot that he got away with remarkable quickness and a slapshot which had the force and accuracy of a rifle.

Red Wing coach Alex Delvecchio said, "When I see a youngster like Redmond shoot, I'm glad I'm not a goalie. He can do it all, but it's what he does with his shot that makes him a star. He is as accurate a shooter at close range or long range as I've ever seen. The only time he gets erratic is when he gets angry."

Redmond was even accused of shooting for goalies' heads when he was angry. "I guess I get my shots high when I get mad and try to hit them too hard," he said with a laugh. Then more seriously

he added, "I do have a temper I have to try to control."

Shrewd Chicago coach Billy Reay often put Dick Redmond at forward and assigned him to shadow his brother when the Hawks played Detroit. A couple of times they slashed at each other with their sticks and swung at each other with their fists. Dick, who had bounced from Minnesota to California to Chicago, said, "When we're on the ice together, we're out to do a job on each other for our teams." But off the ice, they remained buddies.

Off the ice, Redmond was a reserved sort. He wore stylish clothes away from the arena, but at the apartment he shared with a teammate, he favored boots, blue jeans and a windbreaker. He had a country way about him and looked like a cowboy.

"During the season, the team travels so much I like to kick off my shoes and just relax when we're at home. The only time I go out is when I have a date or a game to play," he said. "But then in the off-season I can't seem to relax. I'm used to being on the move, so I get going again."

One summer he visited the Bahamas and Bermuda, then crisscrossed the continent twice, from Florida west to California, then up to Vancouver and back east to Montreal.

In season or out, however, Redmond was serious about his hockey, working to increase his strength, improve his game and sharpen his shot. And his hard work had brought results. Looking back on his accomplishments on the ice and his good times off the ice, he broke into a big grin. "Practice pays off," he said.

J. C. Tremblay

Quebec Nordique defenseman J. C. Tremblay takes the puck in front of his own goal.

In the mid-1970s Jean Claude Tremblay was playing 45 minutes a game for the Quebec Nordiques in the World Hockey Association, a veteran on a new team in the capital of French-speaking Quebec province. The team was poor, finishing out of the league playoffs each of its first seasons. But Tremblay (often known as J.C.) was the best defenseman in the WHA, and he was playing for more than $100,000 a year. He was the reliable anchor of the club, succeeding with a losing team as surely as he had for the champion Montreal Canadiens.

Tremblay was a defenseman—and at Montreal he had been one of the best, though most underrated, in hockey. He was neither a flashy high-scoring defenseman like Bobby Orr nor a rugged defensive specialist like Terry Harper. J.C. played the position with finesse and phenomenal stickwork, complementing Montreal's strong, swift forward lines and helping the French-Canadian team to six regular-season titles and five Stanley Cups in a dozen years.

Born January 22, 1939, in Bagotville, Quebec, a town of 8,000 persons almost 400 miles north of Montreal, J.C. Trem-

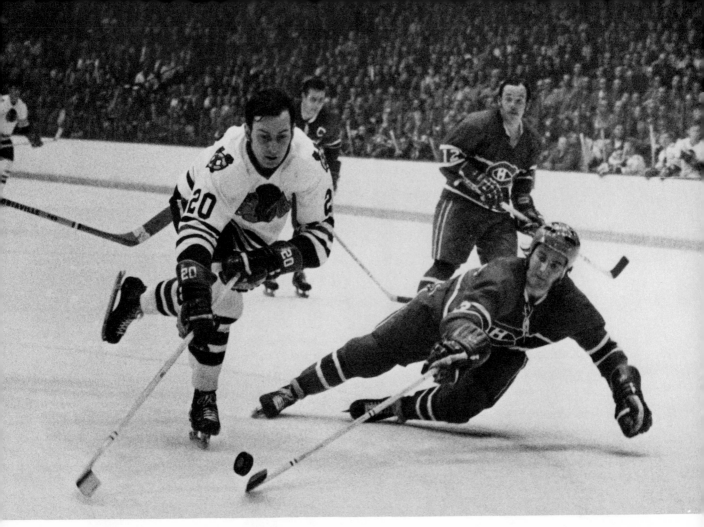

Playing for Montreal, Tremblay knocks the puck away from Chicago's Cliff Koroll.

blay (pronounced *Trom-BLAY*) grew up listening to hockey broadcasts from Montreal, and rooting for the Canadiens.

"I had my heroes," he recalled. "First there was Rocket Richard. I guess he was every kid's hero in those days. Then there was Jean Beliveau, who had his followers. Doug Harvey, of course, was my ideal defenseman."

The eldest of eight children, he was small and a slow skater as a boy. However, he wanted to play very much and worked at it. When he got to the Hull-Ottawa amateur team of the Ontario Hockey Association he was shifted from forward to defense, and he found him-

self. He turned pro with the Hull-Ottawa pro team in the Eastern League in the 1959-60 season, scored 25 goals and was voted most valuable player. Midway in his second season there he was moved to the Montreal team.

In a dozen seasons with the Canadiens he made 57 goals, 306 assists and 363 points in 794 regular-season games. In 108 playoff games he added 14 goals, 51 assists and 65 points.

His specialty was stickwork, and he was a treat to watch. With a swift stab of his stick, he poked the puck off a foe's stick, pulled it in on his own stick and headed down-ice. He skated at top speed, nursing the puck on his stick ahead of him as though the puck were on a rubber band. He made magic with it.

He had marvelous moves. Sometimes he would show the puck to the defender on his left side, faking a pass, then cradle it right and race around the opponent to the right. He was even known to shove the puck between the legs of his foe, then swiftly circle him to pick up his own pass.

He drew defenders to him, freeing a forward. Then with a quick snap of his wrist he flicked a pass to the streaking teammate. If the defender warily laid back to cut off the forward, Tremblay cut in on net himself.

Hockey is at once the fastest and most brutal of team sports. Amazing skaters straight ahead, sideways or backwards, the players cross the shiny white ice at stunning speed. Colliding at top speed, using sticks as weapons, and sometimes using their fists, the participants know that the game can be cruel and unforgiving. But with one like Tremblay, given more to trickery than to toughness, more to grace than collision, the game was also beautiful. Tremblay was a poet of a player.

He made mistakes because his style was a risky one. He seldom tried to drive a forward out of the play physically. Instead, he seemed to give the opponent room to go by, providing an inviting opening, then counted on stealing the puck with a swift stab of his stick. When he missed, the opponent went by him and was in on goal, making Tremblay look bad.

In his early seasons in the majors J.C. missed too often and was booed by the fans. But as he developed he made the play more consistently. Toe Blake, his former coach with the Canadiens, commented, "Over the long run, Tremblay has been brilliant. Add up his plusses and minuses and he comes out far ahead. He has been one of the most brilliant of defensemen."

The Canadiens featured lightning-like forwards such as Yvan Cournoyer and Jacques Lemaire who could drive suddenly into the opposing zone. With them, a defenseman such as Tremblay who could steal the puck and make the perfect pass was invaluable.

He was especially effective in the playoffs. He led the 1965 playoff playmakers with nine assists, making marvelous scoring plays for Cournoyer, Henri Richard and big Jean Beliveau. Montreal won its first Stanley Cup in five seasons.

In 1968, late in the final game of the final series, Tremblay cut across the crease and scooped the puck past the great goaltender Glenn Hall for the winning goal in a 3-2 thriller that brought the precious Cup back to Montreal.

Perhaps his finest season was 1970-71. The Canadiens finished only third. Tremblay had 11 goals and 52 assists during the regular season and was named first All-Star on defense. But it was in the playoffs that he really excelled.

The Boston Bruins had won the Cup in 1970 and had won the pennant in '70-71. Led by Bobby Orr and Phil Esposito, they were heavily favored to defeat the Canadiens in the opening round of the playoffs. They won the opener 3-1, and took a 5-1 lead in the second game. They seemed about to blow the Canadiens right out of the running.

But Montreal mounted a magnificent rally in the second half of the game. Again and again, Tremblay stole the puck from Esposito and Orr. The other Canadiens checked the Bruins relentlessly and stopped them cold. And with Beliveau leading the way with two scores, the offense got hot and came from behind for a 6-5 victory on enemy ice. But Boston bounced back to win two of the next three games to take a lead of three victories to two. Now Montreal had to sweep the last two to survive the series.

In the sixth game, at the Montreal Forum, Tremblay stole the puck and passed it to Frank Mahovlich for the first goal. Phil Esposito tied it for Boston, but Henri Richard put Montreal ahead again before the first period expired.

Midway in the middle period, Boston drew a penalty and Montreal put on its power play with Tremblay on the left point. Handling the puck with his amazing skill, he fed Mahovlich who passed the puck on to Lemaire who lashed it home. Four minutes later, Tremblay himself slashed in and fired the puck past Gerry Cheevers. The Canadiens were on their way to an 8-3 victory.

The seventh game was in Boston. It was 1-1 late in the first period when Tremblay picked off an enemy pass and led Mahovlich with a pass. Frank fed Rejean Houle, who flicked in the lead goal. Late in the period, Tremblay unleashed a slapshot from 30 feet out that flew right past Cheevers. It proved to be the winning score as the Canadiens came out on top 4-3.

In the semi-finals against Minnesota, Tremblay had a goal and five assists in the Canadiens' four winning games.

Behind his own net, Tremblay gets ready to speed down the ice with the puck.

Now they had qualified for the finals against a strong, determined Chicago Black Hawk team.

The series opened at Chicago. Game one was a tense, scoreless struggle until Tremblay picked off a pass, and fed a pass to Lemaire for the lead goal in the second period. However, the Black

140

Hawks bounced back to tie the game, then won it in overtime.

In the second game, the Hawks held a 1-0 lead before Tremblay's passes to Lemaire and Pete Mahovlich produced a 2-1 edge for the Canadiens. Chicago rallied with two to regain the lead, at 3-2, after two periods.

Then, J.C. made two bad moves. First, he cleared a puck carelessly. Instead of controlling it, he got rid of it, belting it into the boards. Lou Angotti grabbed the rebound and raced in to beat Montreal goalie Ken Dryden to make it 4-2 Chicago with twelve minutes left to play. Within two minutes, Frank Mahovlich had cut the count to 4-3. Then, as Tremblay was trying to skate the puck out of his end, Angotti picked the puck off his stick and turned the steal into a score. The Canadiens were beaten 5-3, and Tremblay was the goat.

In the dressing room later, Tremblay was surrounded by the critical Montreal reporters. He stood up to them unflinchingly: "I made two mistakes. It cost us the game. The loss, she is my fault."

He did not make any more mistakes that series. He played with superb concentration the rest of the way. He played careful defense, picking the puck off foes' sticks, and clearing it carefully. Montreal won two at home, then Chicago won again. But the Canadiens won the last two to capture the Cup. In the last contest the Canadiens protected a 3-2 lead for more than 17 minutes. Tremblay, who had key steals from Bobby Hull, Dennis Hull and his old antagonist Angotti, was outstanding. When the buzzer blew, some thought Tremblay would be named the most valuable player of the playoffs,

but the vote went to the Montreal goalie, Ken Dryden.

The following season, Jean Claude was playing at his peak. He scored six goals and assisted on 51 during the season. After the season, the new Nordiques came up with an offer Tremblay could not refuse, and he went over to the newborn team in a new league.

He had no Cournoyers or Lemaires here. His team was weak and did not qualify for the playoffs. But Tremblay was tremendous. His passes were so sure they produced 75 goals from ordinary performers. And he himself scored 14 goals. He won all honors for defensemen.

Tremblay chats with Winnipeg's Bobby Hull.

"It was easy to take their offer since it meant staying in Quebec," J.C. explained. "My wife, Nicole, and my two youngsters don't speak English. It would be hard on them elsewhere. It was hard on me here only because we were losers and I was used to being on winners. Our Coliseum was seldom crowded and I was used to playing in a filled Forum. The atmosphere was so different. But the league will grow, enthusiasm will grow and our team will grow.

"I gave them everything I had. I always work out, off-season as well as in. I take a lot of pride in conditioning myself. I played a lot, but I was doing what I like to do. Once you pass 30 you have to pace yourself some. I couldn't check as hard because that takes too much out of you, but I picked my spots. I'm more of a stick-checker than a body-checker, anyway. Personally, it was a satisfying season. If the team becomes a contender, I will be content."

He was a straight sort of person, spending most of his time off ice with his wife and children. "I am not much of, how you say, a swinger?" he said. "I get my excitement from the games."

Many believed that Tremblay was not recognized for his talent. But when a French-Canadian is a star in Quebec, he gets his share of attention. Tremblay particularly recalled what happened when he helped win the Stanley Cup in 1965. When he returned to Bagotville, he recalled, "I found myself a kind of folk hero in my town. People came from miles around and gathered in front of my house. They organized a big parade that went from my front door to the City Hall about 12 miles away. There, the Mayor was waiting for me. I was presented a beautiful trophy and he declared it 'J.C. Tremblay Day.' I cannot forget it."

If the hockey critics have ignored J.C., they could take a lesson from the enthusiasm of his hometown supporters.

Garry Unger

Garry Unger was the image of the modern hockey hero. Good-looking and rosy-cheeked, he wore his blond hair shoulder length, used a hair drier (which drove the old trainers up a wall)and dressed in colors that would cause a rainbow to blush.

One night after a game, he put on an orange shirt and used a yellow, blue and orange scarf for a tie. He pulled on grey, black and yellow checked bell-bottom slacks, then a sports coat as blue as the Gulf Stream. He stepped into shiny brown cowboy boots. And to top it off he added a brown floppy hat that he'd bought that very day. It looked like it belonged to a cowboy down on his luck.

"Bright colors make me feel happy," he said. "I wouldn't wear a black suit unless I was going to a funeral."

When he played and lived in Detroit, he not only wore fancy clothes, he drove fast cars and dated pretty girls. He dated Miss America in 1970. When someone asked him about her, he said, "She deserves to be a winner." He jokingly added, "She's booked solid most of the year, but I get to date her when she has cancellations."

After moving to St. Louis, Unger changed his style a little. A lover of horses and the great outdoors, Garry hinted to the Blues' wealthy owner he'd like to find a ranch to live on. The owner made available his own little-used 200-acre farm 40 miles from St. Louis. Unger moved right in. There were two houses on the property. The main house had antiques Garry feared he'd break, so he settled into the guest house which had a pool table, a stereo set and a swimming pool. Outdoors he took care of his nine horses, three cats and two dogs, and helped the caretaker with the owner's horses. Garry had begun to breed horses and wanted to have a quarter-horse ranch of his own some day.

Sometimes he drifted into the city for a night on the town, and he found time to sample motorcycling, mountain climbing and water-skiing. He wanted to learn to sky-dive. Once during the off-season he decided to drive cross-country in a convertible with the top down. When it rained heavily the last leg of the journey, he decided to get wet rather than break

Garry Unger seems pleased with his pretty girlfriend and his brightly colored clothes.

his record of having the top down all the way. He was somewhat the worse for the wear, but he said, "It gave me a sense of accomplishment."

Unger's success had come from hockey. But for a long time he had seemed a very unlikely candidate for success. He was born Garry Douglas Unger, December 7, 1947, in Edmonton, Alberta. His father was a career man in the Canadian Army who used to take Garry to see the famed Edmonton Oil Kings play. "My dad took me to games when I was only five or six years old and when he saw I liked hockey, he built a rink in our backyard for me," Garry recalled. "He bought a pair of skates for me, but they were white —girls' skates—so I painted them black."

Garry, who had a younger brother and younger sisters, began his competitive

On the ice, Garry became a major star for the St. Louis Blues.

career in the North Edmonton House League. When his father was transferred to Calgary, Garry played for the South Calgary Community League. He was small and when he went out for bantam hockey, he was cut from the team five times. But he kept sneaking back to try out again and finally was given a place. Soon he was a star scoring leader of a championship team. His coach, a former Toronto player who scouted for the Leafs, offered Garry a spot with the famous St. Michaels School in Toronto. But Garry's parents thought he was too young at 13 to go so far from home. A couple of years later he did try out for St. Mike's, but was cut and assigned to the lesser London Nationals. Before he left Toronto he tried to get a ticket to a Leafs game. No seats were available, but he finally begged a place on the Leafs' bench. It was from there he saw his first big league game.

In 1966-67, he scored 38 goals for London in the OHA amateur circuit and even scored two goals in a two-game tryout with the Tulsa Oilers of the professional Central League. The next season, he was scheduled to try out for the Leafs' top amateur team, the Toronto Marlboros. But the day before the tryout, he injured his left leg clowning around an Ottawa country club. He saw a doctor, who examined the leg and announced that Garry might never play hockey again. Alarmed, Garry ran away, checked into a motel and soaked his sore knee in hot water all night, trying to get it ready for the next day's tryouts. He still couldn't straighten it out the next morning, so with a heavy heart he reported the injury to Toronto and was put in the hospital for the required surgery. He returned to Calgary

to begin the ordeal of recovery. Amazingly, one month after the operation, he was back in action.

The 1967-68 season was a nightmare for Garry. Although his leg was mended and he felt ready to play good hockey, he was sent to five different teams that one season. He started with London in the OHA for two games, turned pro with Tulsa in the Central League for nine games, was sent to Rochester in the American League for five games, then called up to Toronto in the National League for 15 games. "My suitcase was my best friend. I was shook up all the time," he said. He was still only 20 years old. He scored only one goal in his 15 games with the Leafs and on that basis they seem to have given up on him. In March he was traded with Frank Mahovlich and Pete Stemkowski to Detroit in exchange for Carl Brewer, Norm Ullman, Paul Henderson and other players. He finished the long season with 13 games as a Red Wing.

The next season he got 24 goals for the Red Wings and in 1969-70 he scored 42. He was just becoming a star in Detroit when the Red Wings hired a new coach, Ned Harkness, a stern taskmaster from the college ranks. Harkness ordered Garry to cut his shoulder-length hair and Unger refused, one of the reasons Harkness traded him. "This is the style today," Unger pointed out. "If the style tomorrow is short hair and I turn to it, would he ask me to grow my hair long again? It was silly. The length of a guy's hair has nothing to do with the way he plays hockey." And one thing about Garry Unger—he could play.

Unger went to St. Louis in a deal for Red Berenson, who was the most popu-

Unger fires a shot in the 1974 All-Star game. He won it with a third-period goal.

lar player on the Blues. The ardent St. Louis fans had reason to resent Unger. But after he scored his first St. Louis goal, he flipped the puck over the boards to a little boy at rinkside and won the hearts of the reluctant fans. He scored 36 goals his first full season in St. Louis, broke the Blues' team record with 41 his second and scored 33 his third.

After seven seasons, he was established as a star. He might have been better defensively, and he might have passed more and shot less. But fans loved him for his super shooting. "I never worry about goals," he said. "They've always come easy to me. I can never score too many. Every one is a thrill."

He admitted that fame had come so fast he didn't always know how to handle it. Once he told Detroit writer Joe Falls, "I don't know what to do this summer. Maybe I'll go to Europe or maybe South America. I've always wanted to go there. Or maybe Japan. And I want to go to Florida. I love it there. And I want to get in some surfing in California. And I've got my boat, too, you know. God, there's so much to do!"

However, Garry wouldn't take himself too seriously. One season he endorsed a hockey board game. But the manufacturer spelled his name wrong—"Gary" instead of "Garry." When he noticed, Garry laughed. And he tried to be good to his fans. Remembering that as a boy he had once chased Gordie Howe down a street, then was too scared to say anything when he caught up to him, Garry would stand for an hour signing autographs for boys and make conversation with the shy ones.

It was hard for a young hockey star to keep his feet on the ground. Garry was sometimes brought down to earth by the thought of his sister Carol, a victim of polio. "She wears braces and gets around on crutches," Garry said. "She doesn't complain and handles her life well. What I do is easy for me. What she does is hard. She is the one who deserves praise and respect."

Yet, it was nice to be a hockey hero and to have the fame and excitement that go with being a celebrity. "It's the greatest," Garry once admitted. "I feel sorry for those who don't have it at least once in their lives."

Index

Page numbers in italics refer to photographs.